GERMAN
VOCAB
BUILDER

Harriette Lanzer
Anna Lise Gordon

Oxford University Press 1995

Oxford University Press, Walton Street , Oxford OX2 6DP

Oxford New York
Athens Auckland Bangkok Bombay
Calcutta Cape Town Dar es Salaam Delhi
Florence Hong Kong Istanbul Karachi
Kuala Lumpur Madras Madrid Melbourne
Mexico City Nairobi Paris Singapore
Taipei Tokyo Toronto

and associated companies in
Berlin Ibadan

Oxford is a trademark of Oxford University Press

© Oxford University Press 1995

ISBN 0 19 912208 3

Acknowledgements

The illustrations are by Heinz Keller, and the map by Technical Graphics Department, OUP.

Typeset and designed by Mike Brain, Cumnor, Oxford

Printed in Great Britain

Introduction

· ·

Vocabulary is the key to successful language learning – if you don't know the words, then you can't say anything!

As you make progress in German, you will need to use more and more words. Learning and remembering those words might seem like a never-ending task, but if you spend a little time learning new words on a regular basis, you will soon see great results.

This *German Vocabulary Builder* is divided into 22 units, each covering a different topic area. Each unit helps you learn the relevant vocabulary by:
● providing the words you need to know
● suggesting tips to help you learn that vocabulary (*Lerntip!*)
● giving you activities to practise what you've learned (*Wörterspiel*).
Some units also have a mini-cartoon strip where you can practise set phrases.

Within each unit, the vocabulary has been grouped into sub-sections. You can use the list of contents on pages 6–7 to help you find the section you want to learn.

There are lots of different ways of learning vocabulary and it is important that you discover the methods which suit you best.

Lerntip!
Do you do all your written homework first and leave your vocabulary learning till last? It's probably a good idea to learn your vocabulary first while you're still fresh. Then you can quickly test yourself again when your other homework is finished. If you spend five minutes a day learning vocabulary you could learn as many as 2,000 new words in a year!

When you come across new words, write them down in your vocabulary book – you could write them in alphabetical order, in colour coded lists of *der, die, das* words or maybe it's easier if you write them in a word web like this:

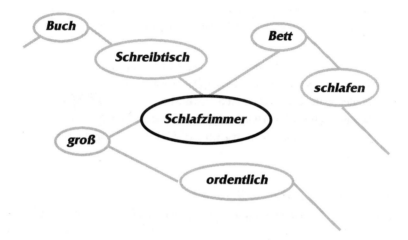

Using this book

● Plural forms are given in brackets after each noun. You add the letters to the end of the noun. If there's an umlaut it goes on the first *a, o,* or *u.*
der Hund (e) = die Hunde
das Haus (¨er) = die Häuser
das Gasthaus (-häuser) = die Gasthäuser

● Separable verbs are marked with / (*an/ziehen*)

● You can find adjectives and verbs listed separately in the final two sections.

● The vocabulary is listed alphabetically with all *der* words given first and then *die* and *das* words following. This is done to help you remember the gender of nouns.

Don't be daunted by how many words there are to learn – concentrate on a small section at a time, learn and practise the vocabulary and when you feel confident with it, move on to another section . . .

Treat vocabulary learning as a priority and watch your German vocabulary increase week by week!

Here are a few ideas for you to try out:

Lerntip!

Carry your vocabulary book around with you wherever you go. You might suddenly have five minutes spare to learn some words – i.e. when the bus is late, the film's boring, you've finished your magazine, etc!

Lerntip!

Record the English and German words from a section of this book on to a cassette. Leave a pause after each English word. You can then play the cassette and say the German word in the pause. As you learn other sections, add them to your cassette. Keep the cassette and listen to it again a few days later, and then a few days after that. If you've got a walkman, you can test yourself on vocabulary wherever you are!

Lerntip!

You don't always have to learn vocabulary on your own! Learn it with a friend and make a game out of it. You each look at a list of words for five minutes. Then you close your books and see who can remember the most words from the list.

Contents

1

Classroom language

●●● *Look at page 39 for ways of saying hello and goodbye!*

asking for help

Was bedeutet das?	What does that mean?
Wie heißt »Fahrkarte« auf englisch?	What's 'Fahrkarte' in English?
Wie sagt man das auf deutsch?	How do you say that in German?
Wie schreibt man das?	How do you write that?
Wie spricht man dieses Wort aus?	How do you pronounce this word?
Können Sie das bitte buchstabieren?	Can you spell that, please?
Können Sie das bitte wiederholen?	Can you repeat that, please?
Können Sie bitte langsamer sprechen?	Can you speak more slowly, please?
Können Sie mir bitte helfen?	Can you help me, please?

asking about the work

Wie macht man diese Übung?	How do you do this exercise?
Was ist die Antwort?	What's the answer?
Ist das richtig oder falsch?	Is that right or wrong?
Du hast recht.	You're right.
Was für eine Note habe ich?	What mark have I got?
Haben wir heute Hausaufgaben?	Have we got homework today?

problems

Wie bitte?	Pardon?
Entschuldigung.	Excuse me.
Ich verstehe nicht.	I don't understand.
Ich kapiere es nicht.	I don't understand it.
Ich weiß es nicht.	I don't know.
Ich habe ein Problem.	I've got a problem.
Ich habe keinen Partner/ keine Partnerin.	I haven't got a partner.

asking for permission

Darf ich das Fenster aufmachen?	Can I open the window?
Darf ich aufs Klo gehen?	Can I go to the loo?
Darf ich bitte einen Kuli leihen?	Can I borrow a pen, please?
Darf ich meine Jacke ausziehen?	Can I take my jacket off?

apologizing

Es tut mir leid, . . .	I'm sorry, . . .
daß ich zu spät komme.	that I'm late.
aber ich habe meine Hausaufgaben nicht gemacht.	but I haven't done my homework.
aber ich habe mein Buch zu Hause gelassen.	but I've left my book at home.
aber ich habe mein Heft verloren.	but I've lost my exercise book.

talking to a partner

Du fängst an.	You start.
Ich bin dran.	It's my turn.
Hör auf!	Stop it!
Ich habe gewonnen!	I've won!
Du mogelst.	You're cheating.
Sei nicht so blöd!	Don't be so stupid!
Das stimmt (nicht).	That's (not) right.
Das macht Spaß.	This is fun.

Los geht's!	Let's start!
Pech!	Bad luck!
Was machen wir jetzt?	What do we do now?
Hören wir jetzt der Kassette zu?	Shall we listen to the tape now?
Fangen wir mit der nächsten Übung an?	Shall we start the next exercise?
Machen wir das zusammen?	Shall we do that together?
Verstehst/Kapierst du das?	Do you understand that?

giving your opinion

Bist du meiner Meinung?	Do you agree with me?
Wie findest du . . .?	What do you think about . . .?
Ich stimme nicht damit überein.	I don't agree with that.
Das finde ich gut/schlecht.	I think that's good/bad.
Meiner Meinung nach . . .	I think that . . .
im Gegenteil	on the contrary

WÖRTERSPIEL

What do you say to your teacher? In German, of course!

a   *You've left your exercise book at home.*
b   *You don't know what the word 'Fußballweltmeisterschaft' means.*
c   *You're late.*
d   *Your teacher is speaking too quickly.*
e   *You want to go to the loo.*
f   *You don't know how to spell 'Bahnhof'.*
g   *You're getting very hot in the classroom.*

2

Numbers, dates and times

die Nummer (n)	number
null	0
eins	1
zwei (zwo *on the phone*)	2
drei	3
vier	4
fünf	5
sechs	6
sieben	7
acht	8
neun	9
zehn	10
elf	11
zwölf	12
dreizehn	13
vierzehn	14
fünfzehn	15
sechzehn	16
siebzehn	17
achtzehn	18
neunzehn	19
zwanzig	20
einundzwanzig	21
zweiundzwanzig	22
dreiundzwanzig	23
vierundzwanzig	24
fünfundzwanzig	25
sechsundzwanzig	26

siebenundzwanzig	27
achtundzwanzig	28
neunundzwanzig	29
dreißig	30
vierzig	40
fünfzig	50
sechzig	60
siebzig	70
achtzig	80
neunzig	90
hundert	100
tausend	1 000
million	1 000 000
hundertdreißig	130
dreitausendneunhundertvierundsechzig	3 964
zweiundzwanzigtausendneunhundertelf	22 911

Lerntip!

Whenever you see a number on a road sign, a bus, a car number plate, a magazine, a shop etc. try and say the number to yourself in German. See how many numbers you can find to say on your way to school. If you are with a friend, see who can say the number first!

der Tag (e)	**day**
Montag	Monday
Dienstag	Tuesday
Mittwoch	Wednesday
Donnerstag	Thursday
Freitag	Friday
Samstag/Sonnabend	Saturday
Sonntag	Sunday
am Montag	on Monday
montags	on Mondays

der Monat (e)	**month**
Januar	January
Februar	February
März	March
April	April
Mai	May
Juni	June
Juli	July
August	August
September	September
Oktober	October
November	November
Dezember	December
im Januar	in January

die Jahreszeit (en)	**season**
der Winter	winter
der Frühling	spring
der Sommer	summer
der Herbst	autumn
im Winter	in winter

das Datum (Daten)	**date**
am ersten Januar	on January 1st
der erste Januar	the 1st of January
zweite (2.)	2nd
dritte (3.)	3rd
vierte (4.)	4th
fünfte	5th
sechste	6th
siebte	7th
achte	8th
neunte	9th
zehnte	10th

elfte	11th
zwölfte	12th
dreizehnte	13th
vierzehnte	14th
fünfzehnte	15th
sechzehnte	16th
siebzehnte	17th
achtzehnte	18th
neunzehnte	19th
zwanzigste	20th
einundzwanzigste	21st
dreißigste	30th

wichtige Daten — important dates

der Feiertag (e)	public holiday
Fasching/Fastnacht	carnival time
Heiligabend	Christmas Eve
Karfreitag	Good Friday
Neujahr	New Year
Ostern	Easter
Pfingsten	Whitsun
Silvester	New Year's Eve
Weihnachten	Christmas

wann? — when?

jetzt	now
heute	today
damals	at that time
gestern	yesterday
vorgestern	the day before yesterday
morgen	tomorrow
übermorgen	the day after tomorrow
am Vormittag	in the morning
am Nachmittag	in the afternoon

am Abend	in the evening
in der Nacht	at night
letzte/nächste Woche	last/next week
unter der Woche	during the week
am Wochenende	at the weekend
am nächsten Tag	on the next day
im Jahre 2011	in 2011
letztes/nächstes Jahr	last/next year
das Jahrhundert (e)	century
bald	soon
dann	then
endlich	at last
nachher	afterwards
plötzlich	suddenly
schließlich	finally
schon	already
seit	since
sofort	immediately
vorher	beforehand
wieder	again
zuerst	at first

wie oft? — how often?

wochentags	on weekdays
werktags	on working days
jeden Tag/täglich	every day/daily
jeden Monat/monatlich	every month/monthly
jede Woche/wöchentlich	every week/weekly
jedes Jahr/jährlich	every year/annually
jedes Wochenende	every weekend
einmal pro Woche	once a week
noch nie	not yet
nicht mehr	no longer
nie	never

selten	rarely
manchmal	sometimes
ab und zu	now and again
gewöhnlich	usually
oft	often
immer	always

die Uhrzeit (en)	**time**
die Sekunde (n)	second
die Minute (n)	minute
die Stunde (n)	hour
früh	early
spät	late
Meine Uhr geht vor/nach.	My watch is fast/slow.

es ist acht Uhr (zwanzig Uhr)	it's eight o'clock (20.00)
es ist fünf vor drei (vierzehn Uhr fünfundfünfzig)	it's five to three (14.55)
um zehn nach vier (sechzehn Uhr zehn)	at ten past four (16.10)
um halb zehn (neun Uhr dreißig)	at half past nine (09.30)
um Mitternacht/Mittag	at midnight/midday

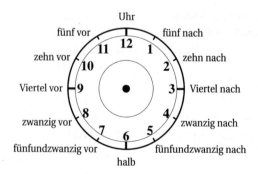

16

Und noch etwas...

fünf vor halb drei — fünfundzwanzig Minuten nach zwei
zehn nach halb elf — zwanzig vor elf
die Hälfte (n) — $\frac{1}{2}$
das Drittel (-) — $\frac{1}{3}$
das Viertel (-) — $\frac{1}{4}$
anderthalb — $1\frac{1}{2}$
zweieinhalb — $2\frac{1}{2}$
das Prozent — %
der Zentimeter (-) — cm
12 minus 5 — 12–5
5 plus 8 — 5 + 8
15 durch 3 — 15 ÷ 3
6 mal 6 macht 36 — 6 x 6 = 36

WÖRTERSPIEL

What comes next? Complete the patterns.

a *zwei, vier, sechs, . . .*
b *Dienstag, Mittwoch, Donnerstag, . . .*
c *April, Mai, Juni, . . .*
d *zwanzig, dreißig, vierzig, . . .*
e *Winter, Frühling, Sommer, . . .*
f *vierte, fünfte, sechste, . . .*
g *Viertel vor sechs, sechs Uhr, Viertel nach sechs, . . .*

Start some other patterns and ask a partner to say what comes next.

Can you say patterns backwards as well? For example, start at *zwanzig* and work your way back to *null*. Or, start with *Sonntag* and get back to *Montag*. How many other patterns can you say backwards?

3

All about me

die Familie (n)	**family**
der Bruder (¨)	brother
der Cousin (s)	cousin (male)
der Enkel (-)	grandson
der Erwachsene (n)	adult
der Freund (e)	friend (male)
der Großvater (-väter)	grandfather
der Herr (en)	man, Mr
der Jugendliche (n)	youth, teenager
der Junge (n)	boy
der Mann (¨er)	husband, man
der Mensch (en)	person, human
der Neffe (n)	nephew
der Onkel (-)	uncle
der Partner (-)	partner (male)
der Pate (n)	godfather
der Schwager (¨)	brother-in-law
der Schwiegervater (¨)	father-in-law
der Sohn (e)	son
der Vater (¨)	father
Vati	dad
der Vetter (-)	cousin
der Zwilling (e)	twin
die Cousine (n)	cousin (female)
die Enkelin (nen)	granddaughter
die Dame (n)	lady
die Frau (en)	wife, woman, Mrs
die Freundin (nen)	friend (female)

die Großmutter (-mütter)	grandmother
die Mutter (¨)	mother
Mutti	mum
die Nichte (n)	niece
die Partnerin (nen)	partner (female)
die Patin (nen)	godmother
die Person (en)	person
die Schwägerin (nen)	sister-in-law
die Schwiegermutter (¨)	mother-in-law
die Schwester (n)	sister
die Tante (n)	aunt
die Tochter (¨)	daughter
das Baby (s)	baby
das Fräulein	Miss
das Kind (er)	child
das Mädchen (-)	girl
das Pflegekind (er)	foster child
das Patenkind (er)	godchild
die Eltern (pl)	parents
die Geschwister (pl)	brothers and sisters
die Großeltern (pl)	grandparents
die Leute (pl)	people
adoptiert	adopted
geschieden	divorced
getrennt	separated
Halb-	half-
ledig	single
Stief-	step-
tot	dead
verlobt	engaged
verheiratet	married
verwitwet	widowed

geboren	to be born
heiraten	to marry
sterben	to die
zusammen/leben	to live together

Und noch etwas...

das Ehepaar (e) — ein Mann und eine Frau, die verheiratet sind
das Einzelkind (er) — ein Kind ohne Geschwister
der Opa/Opi (s) — der Großvater
die Oma/Omi (s) — die Großmutter
der/die Verwandte (n) — jemand in der Familie
die Witwe (n) — der Mann dieser Frau ist tot
der Witwer (-) — die Frau dieses Mannes ist tot

die Charaktereigenschaften — characteristics

die Charaktereigenschaften	characteristics
ängstlich	anxious
arrogant	arrogant
böse	naughty, evil
brav	good, well-behaved
dumm	stupid
ehrgeizig	ambitious
ernst	serious
faul	lazy
fleißig	hard-working
frech	cheeky
fröhlich, glücklich	happy
geizig	greedy
großzügig	generous
gut/schlecht gelaunt	good/bad tempered
hilfsbereit	helpful
intelligent	intelligent
launisch	moody
lebhaft	lively
lustig	funny

nett	nice
nervös	nervous
neugierig	curious
optimistisch	optimistic
pessimistisch	pessimistic
schüchtern	shy
selbständig	independent
selbstsüchtig	selfish
stolz	proud
sympathisch	likeable, kind
tollkühn	daring
traurig	sad
unartig	naughty
(un)ehrlich	(dis)honest
(un)freundlich	(un)friendly
(un)geduldig	(im)patient
(un)höflich	(im)polite
(un)pünktlich	(un)punctual
vernünftig	sensible
verrückt	mad, crazy
zornig	angry
zufrieden	content

das Aussehen (-)	**appearance**
alt	old
attraktiv	attractive
dick	fat
dünn	thin
elegant	elegant
gutaussehend	good looking
häßlich	ugly
hübsch	pretty
jung	young
klein	short, small

groß	tall, big
mager	skinny
mittelgroß	medium height
rundlich	rounded
schlank	slim
schön	beautiful
der Bart (¨e)	beard
der Schnurrbart (-bärte)	moustache
die Brille (n)	glasses
das Gewicht (e)	weight
blondes Haar	blonde hair
dunkel	dark
gefärbt	dyed
glatt	straight
hell	light
kurz	short
lang	long
lockig	curly
die Feier (n)	**party, celebration**
der Geburtstag (e)	birthday
die Bescherung	giving of Christmas presents
die Hochzeit (en)	wedding
die Osterhase	Easter bunny
die Taufe (n)	baptism
das Geschenk (e)	present
feiern	to celebrate
herzlichen Glückwunsch	congratulations

Lerntip!

If you come across a German word that you can't understand, you can look it up in a dictionary or in the alphabetical word list at the back of your course book. If you want to find out the German word for something, use a dictionary – you're not expected to know what everything is in German! As a general rule, the bigger the dictionary, the more helpful it will be.

WÖRTERSPIEL

[**A**] How well do you know the alphabet? Put these words in alphabetical order.

Großvater
Einzelkind
schüchtern
Cousine
Halbbruder
Witwer
intelligent
Stiefbruder
Tante
Enkelin
Religion

What do the words mean in English?

Give your partner a list of 10 words to put in alphabetical order. He/She gives you a list too. Who can sort their list out quickest? Do you know what all the words mean?

[B] Do you understand all the words on this form? Use a dictionary to help you fill it in.

PERSONALAUSWEIS

der Familienname (n) ....

der Vorname (n) ....

das Geschlecht (-)   männlich/weiblich

die Adresse (n) ....

....

....

die Postleitzahl (en) ....

die Telefonnummer (n) ....

das Geburtsdatum (-daten) ....

das Alter (-) ....

der Geburtsort (e) ....

der Wohnort (e) ....

die Staatsangehörigkeit (en)...

die Religion (en)   evangelisch/katholisch

die Unterschrift (en) ....

4

Animals

das Haustier (e) **pet**

1 der Fisch (e)

2 der Hamster (-)

3 der Hund (e)

4 der Papagei (en)

5 der Wellensittich (e)

6 die Katze (n)

7 die Maus (ˇe)

8 die Schildkröte (n)

9 das Kaninchen (-)

10 das Meerschweinchen (-)

das Tier (e)	**animal**
der Elefant (en)	elephant
der Esel (-)	donkey
der Frosch (¨e)	frog
der Fuchs (¨e)	fox
der Kuh (¨e)	cow
der Löwe (n)	lion
der Vogel (¨)	bird
die Affe (n)	monkey
die Ameise (n)	ant
die Biene (n)	bee
die Ente (n)	duck
die Fliege (n)	fly
die Gans (¨e)	goose
die Giraffe (n)	giraffe
die Ratte (n)	rat
die Schlange (n)	snake
die Schnecke (n)	snail
die Spinne (n)	spider
die Ziege (n)	goat
das Insekt (en)	insect
das Huhn (¨er)	chicken
das Känguruh (s)	kangaroo
das Krokodil (e)	crocodile
das Pony (s)	pony
das Pferd (e)	horse
das Schaf (e)	sheep
das Schwein (e)	pig

Lerntip!
Make up rhymes and sentences to help you remember words:
my *Frosch* is posh and my *Biene* is meaner than my fine *Schwein*.

Und noch etwas...

der Zoo (s) — dort leben viele Tiere

der Käfig (e) — kleiner Raum, wo Zootiere leben

die Hundehütte (n) — wo ein Hund schläft

das Futter — das Essen für Tiere

bellen — die »Sprache« eines Hundes

fressen — so essen Tiere

WÖRTERSPIEL

Find an animal word to complete each rhyme. Then link the rhymes to the correct picture.

1   *Ich schlafe auf einer Matratze,*
    Ich bin eine kleine ....

2   *Hier ist ein neues Haus*
    Hier wohnt meine liebe ....

3   *Wie heißt du?*
    Und wie heißt deine schöne ....?

4   *Hast du eine Wiege*
    Für diese dicke ....?

5   *Was ist unter dem Tisch?*
    Ach, nein, das ist mein ....!

Write some more animal rhymes like the ones above. Can your partner find the missing animal in your rhymes?

5

Hobbies

der Sport	sport
Ich spiele gern . . .	I like playing . . .
Badminton, Federball	badminton
Basketball	basketball
Fußball	football
Handball	handball
Hockey	hockey
Kricket	cricket
Netzball	netball
Rugby	rugby
Squash	squash
Streetball	streetball
Tennis	tennis
Tischtennis	tabletennis
Volleyball, Faustball	volleyball
angeln	to fish
joggen	to jog
klettern	to climb
rad/fahren	to cycle
reiten	to ride
rudern	to row
schwimmen	to swim
segeln	to sail
ski/fahren	to ski
Sport treiben	to do sport
tauchen	to dive
trainieren	to train
turnen	to do gymnastics

wandern	to hike
windsurfen	to windsurf
der Platz (¨e)	position, pitch
der Pokal (e)	cup
der Schläger (-)	racket
der Sieger (-)	winner (male)
der Teilnehmer (-)	participant
der Verein (e)	club, organization
der Verlierer (-)	loser (male)
die Siegerin (nen)	winner (female)
die Teilnehmerin (nen)	participant (female)
die Verliererin (nen)	loser (female)
die Weltmeisterschaft (en)	world championship
das Endspiel (e)	final
das Mitglied (er)	member
das Netz (e)	net
verlieren	to lose
gewinnen	to win
spielen	to play

Und noch etwas...

ich bin ein Fan von X — ich finde X fantastisch
der Spieler (-)/die Spielerin (nen) — er/sie spielt
der Schiedsrichter (-) — er kontrolliert das Spiel
der Zuschauer (-) — er sieht sich das Spiel an
der Wassersport — eine Sportart auf dem/im Wasser
der Wintersport — eine Sportart, die man im Winter macht
die Freizeit (en) — die Zeit, in der man nicht arbeitet
die Freizeitbeschäftigung (en) — das Hobby
die Mannschaft (en) — eine Gruppe, die zusammen spielen; z.B. eine
    Fußballmannschaft hat elf Spieler

das Instrument (e)   instrument

1 die Blockflöte (n)
2 die Geige (n)
3 die Gitarre (n)
4 die Klarinette (n)
5 die Oboe (n)
6 die Trompete (n)
7 die Querflöte (n)
8 das Cello (s)
9 das Keyboard (-)
10 das Klavier (e)
11 das Saxophon (e)
12 das Schlagzeug (e)
13 das Orchester (-)

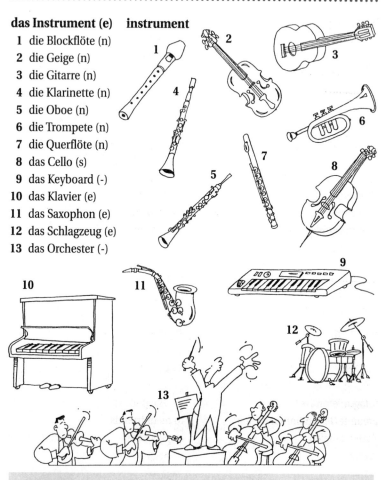

Lerntip!

When you learn a new German noun, remember:

1 what the noun means
2 how you pronounce it
3 how you spell it
4 whether it takes *der, die* or *das*
5 how you make the plural of the noun.

Ich gehe gern . . .

auf Partys	to parties
in die Disco	to discos
ins Einkaufszentrum	to the shopping centre
ins Jugendzentrum	to the youth centre
ins Kino	to the cinema
ins Konzert	to concerts
ins Museum	to the museum
ins Stadion	to the stadium
ins Theater	to the theatre
einkaufen	shopping
Rollschuhlaufen	roller-skating
Schlittschuhlaufen	ice-skating
spazieren	for a walk

I like going . . .

das Hobby (s)

aus/gehen	to go out
basteln	to make things with your hands
bummeln	to wander around town
Computerspiele spielen	to play computer games
faulenzen	to laze around
fern/sehen	to watch TV
fotografieren	to take photos
Freunde/Freundinnen treffen	to meet friends
Karten spielen	to play cards
kochen	to cook
lesen	to read
malen	to paint
Musik hören	to listen to music
Schach spielen	to play chess
schreiben	to write
singen	to sing
stricken	to knit
tanzen	to dance
Telefonkarten sammeln	to collect phonecards

hobby

eine Verabredung machen   to make a date

Can you make up a similar dialogue with a partner?

●●● *Look at page 16 for times and page 63 for some places to meet!*

WÖRTERSPIEL

[A] Tick the correct answer each time.

1 *Du spielst gern in einer Mannschaft. Was machst du gern?*
a *fernsehen* ☐
b *Fußball spielen* ☐
c *Rollschuhlaufen gehen* ☐

2 *Du bist kreativ. Was machst du gern?*
a *malen* ☐
b *klettern* ☐
c *Faustball spielen* ☐

3 *Du liebst Pferde. Was machst du gern?*
a *wandern* ☐
b *turnen* ☐
c *reiten* ☐

4 *Du haßt Musik. Wo gehst du hin?*
a *in die Disco* ☐
b *ins Museum* ☐
c *ins Konzert* ☐

Can you work out some more questions for a partner to answer?

[B] Play this memory game in a group with hobbies you know.

A: *Ich spiele gern Fußball.*
B: *Ich spiele gern Fußball und Badminton.*
C: *Ich spiele gern Fußball, Badminton und Hockey . . .*

A: *Ich spiele gern Fußball.*
B: *Ich spiele gern Fußball, und ich singe gern.*
C: *Ich spiele gern Fußball, ich singe gern, und ich höre gern Musik . . .*

6

At home

das Zimmer (-)	**room**
der Balkon (s)	balcony
der Dachboden (-böden)	attic
der Flur (e)	hall, landing
der Gang ("e)	corridor
der Keller (-)	cellar
der Raum ("e)	room
die Dusche (n)	shower
die Garage (n)	garage
die Küche (n)	kitchen
die Terrasse (n)	terrace
die Toilette (n)	toilet
das Arbeitszimmer (-)	workroom, study
das Badezimmer (-)	bathroom
das Eßzimmer (-)	dining room
das Gästezimmer (-)	guest room
das Kinderzimmer (-)	children's room
das Schlafzimmer (-)	bedroom
das Wohnzimmer (-)	living room
das Haus ("er)	**house**
der Bauernhof (-höfe)	farmhouse
der Bungalow (s)	bungalow
der Wohnblock (-blöcke)	block of flats
die Drei-Zimmer Wohnung (en)	flat with three rooms
die Wohnung (en)	flat
das Doppelhaus (-häuser)	semi-detached house
das Einfamilienhaus (-häuser)	detached house

das Hochhaus (-häuser)	high-rise block
das Reihenhaus (¨er)	terraced house
der Boden (¨)	floor
der (Fenster)laden (-)	shutter
der Kamin (e)	fireplace
der Schornstein (e)	chimney
der Stecker (-)	plug
die Decke (n)	ceiling
die Mauer (n)	wall (outside)
die Treppe (n)	step, stair
die Tür (en)	door
die Steckdose (n)	socket
die Wand (¨e)	wall (inside)
das Dach (¨er)	roof
das Fenster (-)	window
im ersten/zweiten Stock	on the first/second floor

die Möbel (pl)   **furniture**

der Hahn (¨e)	tap
der Herd (e), der Ofen (¨)	oven
der Kleiderschrank (¨e)	wardrobe
der Kühlschrank (¨e)	fridge
der Nachttisch (e)	bedside table
der Papierkorb (-körbe)	wastepaper basket
der Schrank (¨e)	cupboard
der Schreibtisch (e)	desk
der Sessel (-)	armchair
der Spiegel (-)	mirror
der Stuhl (¨e)	chair
der Teppich (e)	carpet, rug
der Tisch (e)	table
der Vorhang (-hänge)	curtain

die Couch (s)	sofa
die Kommode (n)	chest of drawers
die Lampe (n)	lamp
die Mikrowelle (n)	microwave
die Spülmaschine (n)	dishwasher
die Tiefkühltruhe (n)	freezer
die Waschmaschine (n)	washing machine
die Wolldecke (n)	blanket
das Bad (¨er)	bath
das Bett (en)	bed
das Bild (er)	picture
das Bücherregal (e)	bookshelf
das Federbett (en)	duvet
das Kissen (-)	cushion
das Kopfkissen (-)	pillow
das Licht (er)	light
das Regal (e)	shelf
das Sofa (s)	sofa
das Spülbecken (-)	sink
das Waschbecken (-)	basin

Lerntip!

Write the German words from this unit on pieces of card or post-it notes and stick them to the matching objects around your home. Now, wherever you go at home you can learn and remind yourself of these German words!

die Küche (n)   kitchen

1 der Dosenöffner (-)

2 der Korkenzieher (-)

3 der Löffel (-)

4 der Teller (-)

5 der Topf (¨e)

6 die Gabel (n)

7 die Glühbirne (n)

8 die Pfanne (n)

9 die Schüssel (n), die Schale (n)

10 die Tasse (n)

11 die Untertasse (n)

12 das Bügeleisen (-)

13 das Glas (¨er)

14 das Messer (-)

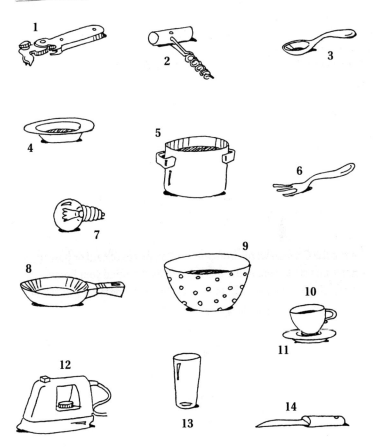

Und noch etwas...

der Nachbar (-)/die Nachbarin (nen) — jemand, der nebenan wohnt
die Eigentumswohnung (en) — eine Wohnung, die einem gehört
die Zentralheizung (en) — Heizung für das ganze Haus
das Besteck — Messer, Gabel und Löffel
das Geschirr — Teller, Schalen, Tassen usw.
das Klo (s) — die Toilette
mieten — man bezahlt jeden Monat Geld, um in einem Haus/einer
    Wohnung zu wohnen
möblieren — Möbel ins Haus einstellen
um/ziehen — man zieht in ein neues Haus

WÖRTERSPIEL

[A] Think of a word to do with the home. Your partner can ask you
    questions to find out your word. You can only answer *ja/nein*. How
    many questions must he/she ask you to guess your word?

Ist es ein Zimmer?	*Beginnt dein Wort mit S?*
Gibt es eins in diesem Zimmer?	*Ist es größer als du?*
Findet man das in der Küche?	*...?...*

[B] Continue this word web. How many words can you think of?

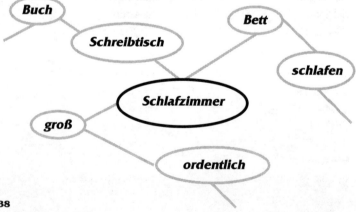

7

Staying with a family

der Gruß (¨e)	**greeting**
hallo	hello
guten Morgen	good morning
guten Tag	hello (during the day)
gute Nacht	good night
grüß dich/euch	hello
servus	hello/goodbye
herzlich willkommen	welcome
komm herein!	come in!
setz dich!	sit down!
Mahlzeit!	hello (around mealtimes)
tschüs	bye
bis später	till later
auf Wiedersehen	goodbye
auf Wiederhören	goodbye (on phone)
schönes Wochenende!	have a good weekend!
mach's gut!	take care!
viel Spaß!	have fun!
alles Gute!	all the best!
Wie geht's (dir/Ihnen)?	How are you?
die Routine (n)	**routine**
auf/wachen	to wake up
auf/stehen	to get up
sich baden	to have a bath
sich duschen	to shower
sich waschen	to wash yourself
sich die Zähne putzen	to brush your teeth

sich das Haar bürsten	to brush your hair
sich an/ziehen	to get dressed
sich um/ziehen	to get changed
sich aus/ziehen	to get undressed
sich rasieren	to shave
frühstücken	to have breakfast
aus dem Haus gehen	to leave the house
zur Schule gehen	to go to school
aus/gehen	to go out
sich aus/ruhen	to rest
ins Bett gehen	to go to bed
ein/schlafen	to go to sleep

Lerntip!

When you learn new words, test yourself on them again a few days later. Write down the words you have forgotten and learn those ones again. Keep doing this and see how soon you can remember all the words.

die Hausarbeit — housework

ab/stauben	to dust
ab/trocknen	to dry up
ab/waschen	to wash up
auf/räumen	to tidy up
backen	to bake
das Bett machen	to make the bed
braten	to fry, roast
bügeln	to iron
einkaufen gehen	to go shopping
grillen	to grill
im Haushalt helfen	to help at home
kehren	to sweep
kochen	to cook
polieren	to polish

putzen	to clean
den Rasen mähen	to mow the lawn
sauber/machen	to clean
schälen	to peel
staub/saugen	to vacuum
den Tisch decken	to lay the table
vor/bereiten	to prepare
waschen	to wash
die Wäsche waschen	to do the washing
wischen	to wipe

am Tisch	**at the table**
Guten Appetit!	Enjoy your meal!
Prost!	Cheers!
Zum Wohl!	Cheers!
Hat's geschmeckt?	Did you like it?
Das schmeckt mir (nicht).	I (don't) like that.
Das war lecker.	That was tasty.
Entschuldigung./Verzeihung.	Excuse me.
Noch Karotten?	More carrrots?
Kriege ich bitte . . . ?	Can I have . . ., please?
Reichst du mir bitte . . .?	Can you pass me . . ., please?
Ja, bitte.	Yes, please.
Nein, danke.	No, thank you.

das Frühstück (e)	breakfast
das Mittagessen (-)	lunch
das Abendbrot (e)	evening meal
das Abendessen (-)	evening meal
die Mahlzeit (en)	meal
das Picknick (s)	picnic

●●● *Look at unit 9 for things to eat and drink!*

Und noch etwas...

der Fön (e) — damit trocknet man die Haare

der Kamm (¨e) — damit kämmt man die Haare

der Rasierapparat (e) — damit rasiert man sich

die Bürste (n) — damit bürstet man die Haare

das Bettzeug (e) — Bettwäsche

der Aufenthalt (e)/der Besuch (e) — wenn man jemanden besucht

der Brieffreund (e)/die Brieffreundin (nen) — man schreibt Briefe an ihn/sie

der Gast (¨e) — eine Person, die zu Besuch ist

das Heimweh — man ist traurig, weil man weg von zu Hause ist

übernachten — man bleibt die Nacht bei jemandem

WÖRTERSPIEL

Fill in the grid to find out what Hänsi does after his daily routine.

der Austausch   exchange

8

At school

das Fach (¨er)	subject
Biologie	biology
Chemie	chemistry
Deutsch	German
Englisch	English
Erdkunde, Geographie	geography
Französisch	French
Geschichte	history
Handarbeiten	textiles
Hauswirtschaft	home economics
Informatik, Computerlehre	computer studies
Italienisch	Italian
Kochen	cookery
Kunst	art
Latein	Latin
Mathe	maths
Musik	music
Naturwissenschaften	science
Physik	physics
Religion	religion
Sozialkunde	social studies
Spanisch	Spanish
Sport	sport
Technik	technology
technisches Zeichnen	technical drawing
Turnen	gym
Wirtschaft	economics

bestehen	to pass (an exam)
durch/fallen	to fail (an exam)
lernen	to learn
schwänzen	to skive
sitzen/bleiben	to repeat a year
studieren	to study

die Schule (n) — school

der Kindergarten (¨)	nursery school
die Berufsschule (n)	vocational school
die Gesamtschule (n)	comprehensive school
die Hauptschule (n)	secondary school
die Realschule (n)	secondary school
die Grundschule (n)	primary school
die Universität (en)	university
das Gymnasium (Gymnasien)	grammar school
das Internat (e)	boarding school

das Zimmer (-) — room

der Computerraum (-räume)	computer room
der Gang (¨e)	corridor
der Kunstsaal (-säle)	art room
der Musiksaal (-säle)	music room
der Schulhof (-höfe)	playground
der Umkleideraum (-räume)	changing room
die Aula (Aulen)	hall
die Bibliothek (en)	library
die Kantine (n)	canteen
die Sporthalle (n)	sports hall
die Toilette (n)	toilet
die Turnhalle (n)	gym
das Klassenzimmer (-)	classroom
das Labor (e)	laboratory
das Lehrerzimmer (-)	staff room

45

das Sekretariat (e)	office

die Leute (pl) — **people**

der Assistent (en)	assistant (male)
der Direktor (-)	headmaster
der Klassenlehrer (-)	tutor (male)
der Lehrer (-)	teacher (male)
der Schüler (-)	pupil (male)
der Student (en)	student (male)
die Assistentin (nen)	assistant (female)
die Direktorin (nen)	headmistress
die Klasse (n)	class
die Klassenlehrerin (nen)	tutor (female)
die Lehrerin (nen)	teacher (female)
die Schülerin (nen)	pupil (female)
die Studentin (nen)	student (female)

Und noch etwas...

der Stundenplan (-pläne) — ein Plan mit den täglichen Stunden
die Fremdsprache (n) — Spanisch, Italienisch, Deutsch, usw.
die Klassenfahrt (en) — ein Ausflug oder eine Reise mit der Klasse
die Nachhilfe — extra Unterricht zu Hause
die Note (n) — z. B. C+ oder 8/10
die Oberstufe (n) — die ältesten Klassen in der Schule
die Mittagspause (n) — die freie Zeit mittags
die Prüfung (en) — das Examen
das Abitur — deutsche Prüfung in der Oberstufe
das Zeugnis (se) — Noten, für jeden Schüler am Ende des Semesters
die Hausaufgaben (pl) — Schularbeit, die man zu Hause macht
hitzefrei haben — es ist so heiß, daß die Schule geschlossen ist
die Versammlung (en) — wenn die Schüler am Anfang des Tages zusammen
   in der Aula sitzen

die Mappe (n)   school bag

1 der Bleistift (e)
2 der Filzstift (e)
3 der Füller (-)
4 der Kugelschreiber (-)
5 der Radiergummi (s)
6 die Diskette (n)
7 das Buch ("er)
8 das Etui (s)
9 das Heft (e)
10 das Lineal (e)
11 das Papier (e)

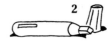
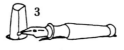

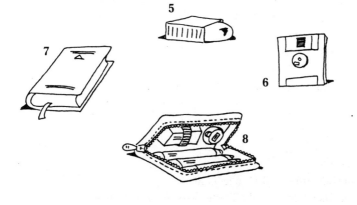

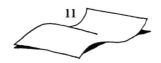

> **Lerntip!**
>
> Try and find words to learn in pairs. You can save yourself time that way:
>
> *die Turnhalle/die Sporthalle*
>
> *das Klassenzimmer/das Lehrerzimmer.*

WÖRTERSPIEL

Can you find fifteen school words in this wordsearch? Write them out. (Try and write them with *der/die/das* and their plural form too.)

```
K  U  G  E  L  S  C  H  R  E  I  B  E  R
L  K  H  R  G  G  H  R  E  W  S  X  V  G
A  F  G  D  E  C  H  E  M  I  E  G  V  F
S  I  Y  K  S  W  S  C  H  U  L  H  O  F
S  L  W  U  A  A  H  K  O  L  K  U  O  P
E  Z  D  N  M  N  K  L  M  I  U  G  L  K
N  S  D  D  T  N  M  J  A  J  N  U  I  L
Z  T  I  E  S  T  W  Q  T  T  S  W  N  A
I  I  R  Y  C  P  L  J  H  O  T  A  E  S
M  F  E  U  H  U  N  V  E  B  C  X  A  S
M  T  K  W  U  B  C  Z  E  M  I  P  L  E
E  P  T  L  L  E  H  R  E  R  I  N  K  J
R  I  O  T  E  U  G  L  A  B  O  R  Y  E
O  R  R  Y  E  W  S  P  O  R  T  K  Y  W
```

What do the words mean in English?

Make up a school wordsearch for a partner to solve.

9

Food and drink

das Obst	fruit
der Apfel (¨)	apple
der Pfirsich (e)	peach
die Ananas (-)	pineapple
die Apfelsine (n), die Orange (n)	orange
die Aprikose (n)	apricot
die Banane (n)	banana
die Birne (n)	pear
die Erdbeere (n)	strawberry
die rote/schwarze Johannisbeere (n)	red/blackcurrant
die Himbeere (n)	raspberry
die Kirsche (n)	cherry
die Kiwi (s)	kiwi
die Melone (n)	melon
die Pampelmuse (n)	grapefruit
die Pflaume (n)	plum
die Tomate (n)	tomato
die Traube (n)	grape
die Zitrone (n)	lemon
das Gemüse (-)	**vegetable**
der Blumenkohl (e)	cauliflower
der Champignon (s), der Pilz (e)	mushroom
der Knoblauch	garlic
der Kohl (e)	cabbage
der Mais	corn
der Paprika (s)	pepper
der Rosenkohl (e)	sprout

der Salat (e)	lettuce
der Spargel (-)	asparagus
die Aubergine (n)	aubergine
die Bohne (n)	bean
die Erbse (n)	pea
die Gurke (n)	cucumber
die Karotte (n)	carrot
die Kartoffel (n)	potato
die Olive (n)	olive
die Salzkartoffel (n)	boiled potato
die Zucchini (-)	courgette
die Zwiebel (n)	onion
das Radieschen (-)	radish
das Sauerkraut	pickled cabbage

Lerntip!

You don't always have to write words down like they are here. Why not write them in shapes? It might help you to remember them!

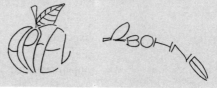

das Getränk (e) — drink

der Alkohol	alcohol
der Kaffee	coffee
der Kakao (s)	cocoa
der Tee	tea
der Saft (¨e)	juice
der Schnaps (¨e)	schnapps
der Sekt (e)	sparkling wine
der Sprudel	sparkling mineral water
der Wein (e)	wine

die Cola (s)	cola
die Limonade (n)	lemonade
die Milch	milk
die heiße Schokolade	hot chocolate
die Schorle (n)	spritzer
die Spirituose (n)	spirit
das Bier (e)	beer
das Mineralwasser	mineral water
das Pils	pils
das Wasser	water

das Frühstück (e) — **breakfast**

der Honig	honey
der Keks (e)	biscuit
der Kuchen (-)	cake
der Pumpernickel (-)	pumpernickel bread
der Toast	toast
der Zucker	sugar
die Butter (-)	butter
die Margarine (n)	margarine
die Marmelade (n)	jam

belegtes Brot	open sandwich
das Brot (e)	bread
das Brötchen (-)	roll
das Butterbrot (e)	buttered bread
ein gekochtes Ei	boiled egg
das Knäckebrot (e)	crispbread
das Müsli (s)	muesli
das Roggenbrot (e)	rye bread
das Rührei (er)	scrambled egg
das Schwarzbrot (e)	dark bread
das Spiegelei (er)	fried egg

das Hauptgericht (e) — main course

das Hauptgericht (e)	**main course**
der Auflauf (-läufe)	soufflé
der Aufschnitt	cold meats
der Eintopf (¨e)	stew
der Essig (e)	vinegar
der Fisch (e)	fish
der Hamburger (-)	hamburger
der Käse (-)	cheese
der Knödel (-)	dumpling
der Lachs (e)	salmon
der Quark ·	quark (soft cheese)
der Pfeffer	pepper
der Reis	rice
der Schinken (-)	ham
der Senf	mustard
der Thunfisch	tuna
die Bockwurst (-würste)	large frankfurter
die Currywurst (-würste)	curried sausage
die Gulaschsuppe (n)	goulash soup
die Forelle (n)	trout
die Frikadelle (n)	rissole
die Leberwurst	liver sausage
die Nudel (n)	pasta
die Soße (n)	sauce
die Suppe (n)	soup
die Wurst (¨e)	sausage
das Ei (er)	egg
das Fleisch	meat
das Hähnchen (-)	chicken
das Kalbfleisch	veal
das Kotelett (s)	cutlet
das Lammfleisch	lamb
das Omelett (s)	omelette

das Rindfleisch	beef
das Salz	salt
das Schnitzel (-)	pork/veal cutlet
das Schweinefleisch	pork
das Steak (s)	steak
die Chips (pl)	crisps
die Kräuter (pl)	herbs
die Meeresfrüchte (pl)	seafood
die Pommes frites (pl)	chips

der Nachtisch (e)	**dessert**
der Apfelstrudel (-)	apple strudel
der Joghurt (s)	joghurt
der Käsekuchen (-)	cheesecake
der Pfannkuchen (-)	pancake
der Pudding (e/s)	blancmange
der Stollen (-)	fruit loaf (at Christmas)
die Nuß (Nüsse)	nut
die Praline (n)	praline
die Schlagsahne	cream
die Schokolade (n)	chocolate
die Torte (n)	gateau
das Apfelmus	stewed apple
das Bonbon (s)	sweet
das Eis (-)	ice cream
das Kompott (e)	stewed fruit
köstlich	delicious
lecker	tasty
salzig	salty
sauer	sour
scharf	sharp
süß	sweet

Und noch etwas...

ich habe Durst — ich will etwas trinken
ich habe Hunger — ich will etwas essen
ich bin allergisch gegen . . . — ich kann . . . nicht essen
ich bin satt — ich bin voll
alkoholfrei — ohne Alkohol
entkoffeiniert — ohne Koffein
das schmeckt gut — das ist lecker
gesund/ungesund — gut/schlecht für den Körper
vegetarisch — man ißt kein Fleisch
indisches/chinesisches Essen — das Essen aus Indien/China

das Restaurant (s)	**restaurant**
der Ruhetag (e)	day when closed
der Stammtisch (e)	usual table
der Vegetarier (-)	vegetarian (male)
die Bedienung	service
die Nachspeise (n)	dessert
die Rechnung (en)	bill
die Speisekarte (n)	menu
die Vegetarierin (nen)	vegetarian (female)
die Vorspeise (n)	starter
die Weinliste (n)	wine list
das Gericht (e)	dish
das Menü (s)	set menu
das Trinkgeld (er)	tip
bedienen	to serve
bestellen	to order
zahlen	to pay

im Café   at the café

Can you make up a café scene with a partner?

WÖRTERSPIEL

[A] Fill in the missing letters for each word. Which fruit can you then make out of the letters?

P A M — E L M U S E
— E I S
T — R T E
P F I R — I C H
M — L C H
S C H I N — E N
— I N T O P F
S — U E R K R A U T

Now see if you can find a vegetable from these missing letters.

K A K A —
S U P P —
S C H — I T Z E L
— O N I G
T R A U — E

Make up a similar puzzle for your partner to solve.

[B] With a small group, choose a category from this section, i.e. meat, vegetables, fruit, etc. Go round the group taking it in turns to name an item from the chosen category. Who can keep going the longest?

A: *Obst*

B: *Himbeere*

C: *Kiwi*

D: *Melone . . .*

10

Shopping

das Geschäft (e)	**shop**
der Friseursalon (s)	hairdresser
der Getränkemarkt (¨e)	drink store
der Juwelier (e)	jeweller
der Kiosk (s)	kiosk
der Markt (¨e)	market
der Supermarkt (-märkte)	supermarket
der Waschsalon (s)	launderette
der Zeitungskiosk (s)	newspaper stand
die Apotheke (n)	chemist (pharmacy)
die Bäckerei (en)	baker
die Boutique (n)	boutique
die Buchhandlung (en)	bookshop
die Drogerie (n)	chemist
die Metzgerei (en)	butcher
das Blumengeschäft (e)	flower shop
das Elektrogeschäft (e)	electrical shop
das Kaufhaus (-häuser)	department store
das Lebensmittelgeschäft (e)	grocer
das Musikgeschäft (e)	music shop
das Postamt (-ämter)	post office
das Versandhaus (-häuser)	mail order business
das Einkaufen	**shopping**
der Ausverkauf (-käufe)	sale
der Einkaufskorb (-körbe)	shopping basket
der Einkaufswagen (-)	shopping trolley
der Kassenzettel (-)	till receipt

die Auswahl	selection
die Kasse (n)	cash till
die Quittung (en)	receipt
das Sonderangebot (e)	special offer
beschädigt	damaged
günstig, preiswert	good value
kostenlos	free
Geld aus/geben	to spend money
um/tauschen	to exchange
verkaufen	to sell

Und noch etwas...

der Kunde (n)/die Kundin (nen) — jemand, der etwas kauft

der Laden (¨) — das Geschäft

der Sommerschlußverkauf (-käufe) — alle Artikel sind dann billiger

die Abteilung (en) — es gibt Abteilungen für Kleider, Getränke, Sportwaren usw. in einem Kaufhaus

das Erdgeschoß (-schosse) — man kommt von der Straße direkt ins Erdgeschoß

das Untergeschoß (-schosse) — der Stock unter dem Erdgeschoß

das Schaufenster (-) — dort kann man die Waren im Fenster sehen

die Geschäftszeiten/die Öffnungszeiten (pl) — wenn die Geschäfte offen sind

Lerntip!

Don't be afraid of long German words! You might think you don't know their meaning, but if you look closely, you'll be surprised. For example, you might not know the word *Blumengeschäft*, but do you know that *Blumen* means 'flowers' and *Geschäft* is 'shop'? If you do, you can work out that *Blumengeschäft* means 'flower shop'!

die Quantität (en)	**quantity**
der Becher (-)	carton
der Liter, l	litre
die Dose (n)	can, tin
die Flasche (n)	bottle
die Pfandflasche (n)	refundable bottle
die Portion (en)	portion
die Schachtel (n)	box
die Scheibe (n)	slice
die Tube (n)	tube
die Tüte (n)	bag
das Gramm, g	gramme
das Kilo, kg	kilo
das Paar (e)	pair
das Päckchen (-)	small packet
das Paket (e)	packet
das Pfund (e)	pound
das Stück (e)	piece
ein bißchen, ein wenig	a little
einige	several
halb	half
viele	many

●●● *Look at unit 9 for food and drink words!*

der Stoff (e)	**material**
aus . . .	made from . . .
Baumwolle	cotton
Gold	gold
Gummi	rubber
Holz	wood
Kunststoff	man-made fibre
Leder	leather

Plastik	plastic
Seide	silk
Silber	silver
Stahl	steel
Wolle	wool

die Kleider (pl) — clothes

der Anorak (s)	anorak
der Anzug (-züge)	suit
der Badeanzug (-züge)	swimming costume
der BH (s)/Büstenhalter (-)	bra
der Gummistiefel (-)	wellington boot
der Gürtel (-)	belt
der Handschuh (e)	glove
der Hausschuh (e)	slipper
der Hut (¨e)	hat
der Jogginganzug (-züge)	tracksuit
der Mantel (¨)	coat
der Minirock (¨e)	miniskirt
der Ohrring (e)	earring
der Pulli (s)	pullover
der Ring (e)	ring
der Rock (¨e)	skirt
der Schal (e)	scarf
der Schlafanzug (-züge)	pyjamas
der Schlips (e)	tie
der Schuh (e)	shoe
der Sportschuh (e)	trainer
der Stiefel (-)	boot
die Badehose (n)	trunks
die Bluse (n)	blouse
die Hose (n)	pair of trousers
die Jacke (n)	jacket
die Jeans (-)	jeans

die Kette (n)	chain
die Krawatte (n)	tie
die Mütze (n)	cap, hat
die Sandale (n)	sandal
die Socke (n)	sock
die Strumpfhose (n)	tights
die Unterhose (n)	underpants
das Hemd (en)	shirt
das Kleid (er)	dress
das T-Shirt (s)	T-shirt
das Unterhemd (er)	vest
die Shorts (pl)	shorts
die Unterwäsche (pl)	underwear

WÖRTERSPIEL

[A] These eight words have been joined together wrongly. Can you work out what they should be?

Jogginganzug, . . .

Jogging/haus
Pfand/kiosk
Super/geschäft
Blumen/stiefel
Gummi/flasche
Kauf/hose
Zeitungs/anzug
Bade/markt

[B] What can you buy in these shops: *Getränkemarkt, Boutique, Metzgerei, Zeitungskiosk, Supermarkt*? Write down as many items as you can think of for each shop – not just words from this unit. Compare your list with a partner's and add any further words to your list.

im Geschäft   at the shop

Can you make up a similar scene with a partner?

11

In town

die Stadt (¨e)	**town**
der Bahnhof (-höfe)	station
der Busbahnhof (-höfe)	bus station
der Campingplatz (-plätze)	campsite
der Dom (e)	cathedral
der Flughafen (-häfen)	airport
der Friedhof (-höfe)	cemetery
der Markt (¨e)	market
die Bank (en)	bank
die Bibliothek (en)	library
die Disco (s)	disco
die Garage (n)	garage
die Imbißstube (n)	snack bar
die Jugendherberge (n)	youth hostel
die Kirche (n)	church
die Kneipe (n)	bar
die Polizeiwache (n)	police station
die Schule (n)	school
die Tiefgarage (n)	underground carpark
das Einkaufszentrum (-zentren)	shopping centre
das Freibad (¨er)	outdoor pool
das Geschäft (e), der Laden (¨)	shop
das Hallenbad (-bäder)	indoor pool
das Hotel (s)	hotel
das Kaffeehaus (-häuser)	coffee house
das Kino (s)	cinema
das Krankenhaus (-häuser)	hospital
das Museum (Museen)	museum

das Postamt (-ämter)	post office
das Rathaus (-häuser)	town hall
das Reisebüro (s)	travel agency
das Restaurant (s)	restaurant
das Schloß (Schlösser)	castle
das Schwimmbad (¨er)	swimming pool
das Stadion (Stadien)	stadium
das Theater (-)	theatre
das Verkehrsamt (¨er)	tourist information

●●● *Look at page 57 for shops!*

> **Lerntip!**
>
> How can I possibly remember whether a word is *der, die* or *das*? Why not put a list of all *der* words in the hallway, *die* words in the kitchen and *das* words in your bedroom? That way you'll be able to look at them whenever you pass by and you can picture which group a word belongs to!

die Richtung (en)   direction

1 links
2 rechts
3 geradeaus
4 die erste Straße rechts
5 die zweite Straße links
6 auf der rechten Seite
7 auf der linken Seite
8 über die Brücke
9 um die Ecke
10 bis zur Ampel

gegenüber von	opposite
neben	next to
hinter	behind
vor	in front of
zwischen	between
gleich daneben	right beside it

auf der Straße   on the street

der Bahnübergang (-gänge)	level crossing
der Bürgersteig (e)	pavement
der Fußgänger (-)	pedestrian
der Kreisverkehr (-)	roundabout
der Park (s)	park
der Platz (¨e)	square
die Ampel (n)	traffic lights
die Bauarbeit (en)	construction work
die Baustelle (n)	roadworks
die Brücke (n)	bridge
die Bushaltestelle (n)	bus stop
die Ecke (n)	corner
die Einbahnstraße (n)	one-way street
die Fußgängerzone (n)	pedestrian zone
die Hauptstraße (n)	main street, High Street
die Kreuzung (en)	crossroads
die Straße (n)	street
die U-Bahn (en)	underground station
die Umleitung (en)	diversion
die Unterführung (en)	underpass
das Denkmal (e)	statue
das Schild (er)	signpost
alle Richtungen	through traffic

Und noch etwas...

der Einwohner (-) — jemand, der dort wohnt

die Grünanlage (n) — Plätze mit Bäumen und Rasen

der Kinderspielplatz (¨e) — ein Gebiet, wo Kinder spielen können

im Zentrum — direkt in der Mitte

der Vorort (e) — ein Wohngebiet etwas außerhalb der Stadt – Kingston ist ein Vorort von London

die Hauptstadt (-städte) — Berlin ist die Hauptstadt von Deutschland

die Großstadt (-städte) — eine Stadt mit vielen Einwohnern

die Sehenswürdigkeiten — sie sind interessant für Touristen

in der Bank / at the bank

in der Bank	at the bank
der Geldautomat (en)	cash point
der Kontoauszug (-züge)	statement
der Kurs (e)	exchange rate
der Pfennig (e)	pfennig
der Reisescheck (s)	travellers cheque
der Scheck (s)	cheque
der Schein (e)	note
deutsche Mark	German mark
die Kreditkarte (n)	credit card
die Münze (n)	coin
die Schuld (en)	debt
die Sparkasse (n)	savings bank
die Währung (en)	currency
die Wechselstube (n)	bureau de change
das Bargeld	cash
das Geld (er)	money
das Kleingeld	change
das Konto (Konten)	account
das Pfund (e)	pound
das Scheckbuch (¨er)	cheque book
das Taschengeld (er)	pocket money

ab/heben	to withdraw
aus/geben	to spend
bar zahlen	to pay in cash
sparen	to save
überweisen	to transfer
wechseln	to change

WÖRTERSPIEL

Look at this picture for 30 seconds. Then close the book and write down as many items from it as you can remember – in German, of course! Open the book again and check that your words really are in the picture.

Try it again in a couple of week's time and see how many items you can remember then!

12

Travel

das Verkehrsmittel (-)	**mode of transport**
der Bus (se)	bus, coach
der Dampfer (-)	steamship
der Hubschrauber (-)	helicopter
der Lastkraftwagen (-)	lorry
der Zug (¨e)	train
die Fähre (n)	ferry
die S-Bahn (en)	city train
die Straßenbahn (en)	tram
die U-Bahn (en)	underground
das Auto (s)	car
das Boot (e)	boat
das Fahrrad (-räder)	bicycle
das Flugzeug (e)	aeroplane
das Luftkissenboot (e)	hovercraft
das Mofa (s)	moped
das Motorrad (-räder)	motorbike
das Schiff (e)	ship
das Taxi (s)	taxi
mit dem Rad fahren	to go by bike
mit der U-Bahn fahren	to go by underground
zu Fuß gehen	to go on foot
unterwegs sein	to be out and about
aus/steigen	to get off
ein/steigen	to get in
reisen	to travel
trampen	to hitch hike

am Bahnhof	**at the station**
der Bahnsteig (e)	platform
der Fahrausweis (e)	travel card
der Fahrkartenschalter (-)	ticket office
der Fahrplan (-pläne)	timetable
der Fensterplatz (¨e)	window seat
der Gepäckträger (-)	porter
der (Haupt)bahnhof (-höfe)	(main) station
der Kontrolleur (e)	ticket inspector
der (Nicht)Raucher (-)	(non)smoker
der Platz (¨e)	seat
der Schlafwagen (-)	sleeping compartment
der Speisewagen (-)	buffet car
der Treffpunkt (e)	meeting point
der Zuschlag (-schläge)	supplement
die Abfahrt (en)	departure
die Ankunft (-künfte)	arrival
die Ermäßigung (en)	reduction
die Fahrkarte (n)	ticket
die Gepäckannahme (n)	left luggage office
eine einfache Karte	single ticket
erster/zweiter Klasse	first/second class
die Linie (n)	line
die Verbindung (en)	connection
die Verspätung (en)	delay
das Abteil (e)	compartment
das Gepäck (-)	luggage
das Gleis (e)	platform
das Schließfach (¨er)	luggage locker
das Wartezimmer (-)	waiting room
die Zugestiegenen (pl)	people who have joined the train
hin und zurück	return

besetzt	occupied
direkt	direct
gültig	valid
planmäßig	scheduled
verspätet	delayed
entwerten	to date-stamp a ticket
reservieren	to reserve
um/steigen	to change
verpassen	to miss
zurück/bleiben	to stand clear

am Schalter   at the ticket office

Can you make up a similar dialogue with a partner?

am Flughafen	**at the airport**
der Abflug (-flüge)	departure
der Flug ("e)	flight
der Kapitän (e)	captain
der Pilot (en)	pilot (male)
der Steward (s)	air steward
der Zoll ("er)	customs duty
die Besatzung (en)	crew
die Bordkarte (n)	boarding card
die Pilotin (nen)	pilot (female)
die Stewardeß (-essen)	air hostess
das Jet-lag	jetlag
an Bord	on board
ein/checken	to check in
fliegen	to fly
landen	to land
starten	to take off

Und noch etwas...

ICE/IC — zwei schnelle Züge

DB — die deutsche Bahn (wie British Rail)

Lkw — ein Lastkraftwagen

Pkw — ein Auto

der Kilometer (-), die Meile (n) — 80km = 50 Meilen

die Geldstrafe (n) — wenn man zu schnell fährt, muß man der Polizei Geld zahlen

die Geschwindigkeit — wie schnell man fährt

die Verkehrspolizei — Polizei, die den Verkehr kontrolliert

der Geisterfahrer (-) — jemand, der in die falsche Richtung auf der Autobahn fährt

die Tempoüberschreitung (en) — wenn man schneller als das Tempolimit fährt

mit dem Auto   by car

1   der Auspuff (e)

2   der Dachträger (-)

3   der Kofferraum (-räume)

4   der Reifen (-)

5   der Scheinwerfer (-)

6   der Scheibenwischer (-)

7   der Sicherheitsgurt (e)

8   die Windschutzscheibe (n)

9   das Kennzeichen (-)

10   das Lenkrad (¨er)

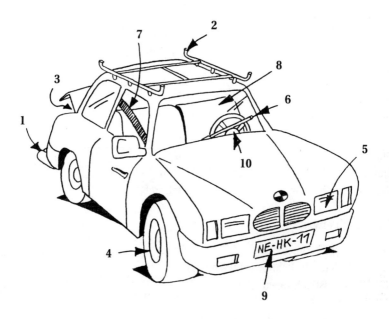

der Diesel	diesel
der Fahrer (-)	driver
der Fahrgast (-gäste)	passenger
der Führerschein (e)	driving licence
der Motor (en)	engine
der Parkschein (e)	parking ticket
der Stau (s)	traffic jam
der Zoll (¨e)	toll
die Ausfahrt (en)	exit (on motorways)
die Autobahn (en)	motorway
die Batterie (n)	battery
die Bremse (n)	brake
die Landstraße (n)	B road
die Raststätte (n)	service area
die Reifenpanne (n)	puncture
die Selbstbedienung, SB	self-service station
die Tankstelle (n)	petrol station
die Vorfahrt (en)	priority
das Benzin	petrol
das Öl	oil
die Parkgebühren (pl)	parking fees
bleifrei	lead free
normal	2-star petrol
super	4-star petrol
verboten	forbidden
tanken	to fill up with petrol
überholen	to overtake
eine Panne haben	to have a breakdown

Lerntip!

Words often come in families and it helps if you can recognize these. For example, you know that *Flug* means 'flight', so *Flugzeug* must have something to do with a flight and so must *Flughafen* and perhaps *fliegen* does too. When you come across new words in texts, look at them carefully – you'll be surprised how many you can recognize from other words.

WÖRTERSPIEL

[A] Can you label these forms of transport?

   a *mit dem Rad*

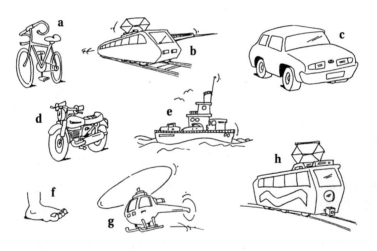

[B] The verbs below are similar to other words from this unit. Can you work out what they mean in English?

verbinden – to connect

a	*rad/fahren*	**e**	*ein/packen*	**i**	*scheinen*
b	*bremsen*	**f**	*schließen*	**j**	*speisen*
c	*lenken*	**g**	*sich verspäten*	**k**	*sichern*
d	*fahren*	**h**	*warten*	**l**	*ab/fahren*

13

On holiday

das Land (¨er)	country
Australien	Australia
Belgien	Belgium
China	China
Dänemark	Denmark
Deutschland	Germany
England	England
Finnland	Finland
Frankreich	France
Griechenland	Greece
Großbritannien	Great Britain
Indien	India
Irland	Ireland
Italien	Italy
Kanada	Canada
die Karibik	Caribbean
Neuseeland	New Zealand
Norwegen	Norway
Österreich	Austria
Polen	Poland
Rußland	Russia
Schottland	Scotland
Schweden	Sweden
die Schweiz	Switzerland
Spanien	Spain
die Türkei	Turkey
Ungarn	Hungary
die Vereinigten Staaten	USA
Wales	Wales
die Kanaren	Canaries

Afrika	Africa
Amerika	America
Asien	Asia
Europa	Europe

die Nationalität (en)	**nationality**
belgisch	Belgian
britisch	British
chinesisch	Chinese
dänisch	Danish
deutsch	German
englisch	English
französisch	French
griechisch	Greek
holländisch	Dutch
indisch	Indian
irisch	Irish
italienisch	Italian
japanisch	Japanese
österreichisch	Austrian
portugiesisch	Portuguese
russisch	Russian
schottisch	Scottish
schweizerisch	Swiss
spanisch	Spanish
türkisch	Turkish

Lerntip!

Have you ever tried to rap vocabulary? It can be a useful way of remembering lists of words, such as countries and nationalities. Get a good rhythm going as you recite the words and you'll find it easier to remember them later on.

Und noch etwas...

die Stadtrundfahrt (en) — eine Tour um eine Stadt
die Bootsfahrt (en) — eine Tour im Boot
ins Ausland fahren — man fährt in ein fremdes Land
der Ausflug (-flüge) — die Reise
die Pauschalreise (n) — eine organisierte Reise mit Unterkunft und Flug
der Tourist (en)/die Touristin (nen) — eine Person, die eine andere Stadt
    oder ein anderes Land besucht
die Sommerferien (pl) — Urlaub im Sommer
besichtigen — besuchen

das Gepäck	**luggage**
der Ausweis (e)	identity card
der Euroscheck (s)	Eurocheque
der (Farb)film (e)	(colour) film
der Fotoapparat (e)	camera
der Koffer (-)	suitcase
der Regenschirm (e)	umbrella
der Reisepaß (-pässe)	passport
der Reisescheck (s)	travellers cheque
der Rucksack (-säcke)	rucksack
der Stadtplan (-pläne)	town plan
die Handtasche (n)	handbag
die Landkarte (n)	map
die Sonnenbrille (n)	sunglasses
die Sonnencreme (n)	suncream
das Adressenbuch (-bücher)	address book
das Portemonnaie (s)	purse
das Tagebuch (-bücher)	diary
das Visum (Visa)	visa
die Kleider (pl)	clothes
ein/packen	to pack
aus/packen	to unpack

am Fundbüro   at the lost property office

Can you make up a similar dialogue with a partner?

DEUTSCHLAND

0   50   100 km
0   25   50   75 Meilen

N
W   O
S

Ostsee

Nordsee

Kiel

SCHLESWIG-
HOLSTEIN

Rostock

MECKLENBURG-
VORPOMMERN

BREMEN

Hamburg   Schwerin

Bremen   HAMBURG

BRANDENBURG

NIEDERSACHSEN

Berlin   BERLIN

Hannover   Magdeburg   Potsdam

SACHSEN-ANHALT

NORDRHEIN-WESTFALEN

Leipzig

Düsseldorf

SACHSEN

Rhein

Erfurt   Dresden

HESSEN   THÜRINGEN   Chemnitz

Mosel

Wiesbaden   Frankfurt

Main

Mainz

RHEINLAND
-PFALZ

Rhein

Nürnberg

Saarbrücken

BAYERN

SAARLAND

Stuttgart

Donau

BADEN-
WÜRTTEMBERG

München   Inn

WÖRTERSPIEL

[A] Look at these towns. In which country would you find each one?

a *Rom*
b *Athen*
c *Hannover*
d *Moskau*
e *München*
f *Wien*
g *Genf*

[B] Look at the map of Germany on page 79. Can you answer these questions?

a *Wie viele Länder gibt es in Deutschland?*
b *In welchem Land ist Stuttgart?*
c *Wie heißt das Land nordost von Niedersachsen?*
d *Ist Bayern im Süden?*
e *Ist Chemnitz in Hessen?*
f *An welchem Fluß liegt Frankfurt?*

Make up some more geography quiz questions for a partner to answer.

14

Accommodation

das Hotel (s)	**hotel**
der Fahrstuhl (-stühle)	lift
der Feuerlöscher (-)	fire extinguisher
der Garten (¨)	garden
der Parkplatz (-plätze)	parking space
der Schlüssel (-)	key
der Seeblick (e)	sea view
die Aussicht (en)	view
die Broschüre (n)	brochure
die Gästekarte (n)	guest card
die Halbpension	half-board
MWSt. = die Mehrwertsteuer	VAT
die Pension (en)	guest house, bed and breakfast
die Preisliste (n)	price list
die Rechnung (en)	bill
die Rezeption (en)	reception
die Sauna (s)	sauna
die Vollpension	full-board
das Doppelzimmer (-)	double room
das Einzelzimmer (-)	single room
das Frühstücksbüfett (s)	breakfast buffet
das Gasthaus (-häuser)	guest house
das Restaurant (s)	restaurant
bequem	comfortable
gemütlich	cosy
(nicht) inklusive	(not) included
klimatisiert	air-conditioned

privat	private
rollstuhlgerecht	with wheelchair access
ruhig	quiet
sauber	clean
schmutzig	dirty
Zimmer frei	rooms available
sich an/melden	to sign in
bestellen, reservieren	to reserve
empfangen	to receive, welcome
leihen	to hire
übernachten	to stay the night

●●● *Look at page 34 for rooms in a hotel!*

> ### Lerntip!
>
> Make a set of picture learning cards. Cut up a piece of card and draw or stick a picture of a vocabulary item on one side of each piece. On the other side, write the German word. You can now look at the picture and say the German word, or look at the German word and name the item. Turn the card over to see if you were right. You can use your picture cards with a partner as well.

Und noch etwas...

der Herbergsvater (¨)/die Herbergsmutter (¨) — der Leiter/die Leiterin einer Jugendherberge

die Hausordnung (en) — die Regeln in einer Jugendherberge

die Übernachtung (en) — die Nacht in einem Hotel, auf einem Campingplatz, usw.

die Reservierung (en) — wenn man vorher ein Zimmer oder einen Platz bestellt

der Campingplatz (-plätze)   **campsite**

1 der Campingkocher (-)
2 der Schlafsack (-säcke)
3 der Rucksack (-säcke)
4 die Batterie (n)
5 die Schlafmatte (n)
6 die Taschenlampe (n)
7 das Taschenmesser (-)
8 das Zelt (e)
9 die Streichhölzer (pl)

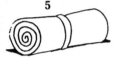

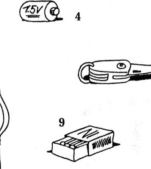

der Klapptisch (-)	foldable table
der Platz (¨e)	site
der Waschraum (-räume)	washroom
der Wohnwagen (-)	caravan
die Luftmatratze (n)	air bed
das Camping	camping
das Lagerfeuer (-)	camp fire
das Trinkwasser	drinking water
auf/schlagen	to put up (tent)

am Empfang   at the reception

Can you make up a similar dialogue with a partner?

WÖRTERSPIEL

[A] Work with a partner. Start spelling a word from this unit – with the German alphabet, of course! How many letters do you need to say before your partner guesses your word correctly and says its English meaning?

[B] Complete the sentences below with a suitable word. There is more than one possible answer each time.

Guten Tag. Ich habe ... reserviert.
Kann ich bitte ... leihen?
Wo finde ich ...?
Gibt es hier ...?
Was kostet ...?
Ist ... inklusive Mehrwertsteuer?

15

The body

der Körper (-)   body

1 der Arm (e)
2 der Daumen (-)
3 der Ellenbogen (-)
4 der Finger (-)
5 der Fuß (¨e)
6 der Hals (¨e)
7 der Mund (¨er)
8 die Hand (¨e)
9 die Nase (n)
10 die Zehe (n)
11 das Auge (n)
12 das Bein (e)
13 das Knie (n)
14 das Ohr (en)

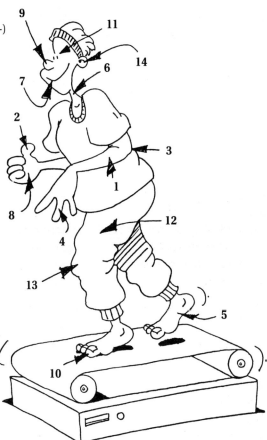

der Atem	breath
der Fingernagel (¨)	fingernail
der Kopf (¨e)	head
der Magen (-)	stomach
der Bauch (¨e)	belly
der Knöchel (-)	ankle
der Hintern (-)/der Po (s)	bottom
der Rücken (-)	back
der Zahn (¨e)	tooth
die Brust (¨e)	breast, chest
die Haut (¨e)	skin
die Schulter (n)	shoulder
die Stimme (n)	voice
die Zunge (n)	tongue
das Gesicht (er)	face
das Herz (en)	heart

die Krankheit (en) — **illness**

der Ausschlag (-schläge)	rash
der Durchfall	diarrhoea
der Heuschnupfen	hay fever
der Insektenstich (e)	insect bite
der Pickel (-)	spot
der Schmerz (en)	pain
der Schnupfen	cold
der Sonnenbrand	sunburn
der Sonnenstich	sunstroke
die Allergie (n)	allergy
gute Besserung!	get well soon!
die Erkältung (en)	chill, cold
die Gänsehaut	goosepimples
die Grippe (n)	flu
die Lebensmittelvergiftung	food poisoning

die Verstopfung	constipation
das Asthma	asthma
die Masern (pl)	measles
die Seitenstiche (pl)	side stitch
allergisch (gegen)	allergic (to)
atemlos	breathless
bewußtlos, ohnmächtig	unconscious
blaß	pale
erschöpft	exhausted
geschwollen	swollen
krank	ill
müde	tired
schmerzhaft	painful
schwindlig	dizzy
seekrank	seasick
verstopft	constipated
Fieber haben	to have a temperature
Kopfschmerzen haben	to have a headache
Magenschmerzen haben	to have stomach ache
husten	to cough
kotzen, sich übergeben	to vomit
niesen	to sneeze
schwitzen	to sweat
weinen	to cry
weh tun	to hurt
mein Bein tut weh	my leg hurts

Lerntip!

Try and find a quiet place to learn your vocabulary. You'll remember more after five minutes concentrated learning than after half an hour with the TV on.

der Unfall (-fälle)	**accident**
der Gips (-)	plaster cast
der Feuerwehrwagen (-)	fire engine
der Krankenwagen (-)	ambulance
der Notfall (-fälle)	emergency
der Notruf (e)	emergency call
den Notruf wählen	to dial 999
der Optiker (-)	optician
der Polizeihund (e)	police dog
der Zusammenstoß (-stöße)	crash
die Feuerwehr (en)	fire brigade
erste Hilfe	first aid
die Krankenkasse (n)	medical insurance
die Narbe (n)	scar
die Operation (en)	operation
die Polizei	police
die Schnittwunde (n)	cut
die Spritze (n)	injection
die Wunde (n)	wound
das Blut	blood
das Krankenhaus (-häuser)	hospital
die Unterlagen (pl)	documents
Feuer!	fire!
Hilfe!	help!
Vorsicht!	careful!
tot	dead
verbrannt	burnt
(schwer) verletzt	(badly) injured
behandeln	to treat
bluten	to bleed
sich den Arm brechen	to break your arm

sich erholen	to recover
ertrinken	to drown
heilen	to cure
pflegen	to look after
retten	to rescue
sterben	to die
töten	to kill
überfahren	to run over
ums Leben kommen	to die
untersuchen	to examine
sich den Fuß verstauchen	to sprain your ankle
verunglücken	to have an accident

die Apotheke (n)   **chemist**

der Tampon (s)	tampon
der Verband (¨e)	bandage
die Damenbinde (n)	sanitary towel
die Impfung (en)	vaccination
die Medizin (en)	medicine
die Pastille (n)	pastille
die Pille (n)	pill
die Seife (n)	soap
die Sonnenbrandcreme (s)	sunburn cream
die Tablette (n)	tablet
die Watte (n)	cotton wool
die Zahnbürste (n)	toothbrush
die Zahnpasta	toothpaste
das Aspirin (s)	aspirin
das Halsbonbon (s)	throat sweet
das Kondom (e)	condom
das Mittel gegen	remedy against
das Pflaster (-)	plaster
das Rezept (e)	prescription

das Thermometer (-)	thermometer
die Antibiotika (pl)	antibiotics
die Tropfen (pl)	drops

Und noch etwas...

blind — man kann nicht sehen
stumm — man kann nicht sprechen
taub — man kann nicht hören
mir ist schlecht — ich bin krank
der Patient (en)/die Patientin (nen) — jemand, der krank ist
Diät machen — man versucht dünner zu werden
schwanger sein — ein Baby erwarten
die Sprechstunde (n) — die Zeit, in der man den Arzt sehen kann
der Rollstuhlfahrer (-)/die Rollstuhlfahrerin (nen) — jemand im Rollstuhl
zu/nehmen — man wird dicker
ab/nehmen — man wird dünner

WÖRTERSPIEL

Monster game (for one or more players)
You need two dice, a piece of paper and a pencil for this game.
Throw the dice and look at the pictures on page 91. Name the part of the body and draw it on your paper. Keep on throwing the dice until you have drawn a monster.
See who can draw the funniest monster!

A: Sieben. Also das ist ein Auge.
B: Vier. Das ist ein Arm.

Score   *Body part*

Can you describe your monster?

Mein Ungeheuer hat drei Köpfe, neun Beine, ein Auge, keine Füße . . .

16

Weather and environment

das Wetter	weather
Es ist . . .	It's . . .
bedeckt	overcast
bewölkt, wolkig	cloudy
feucht	damp
heiß	hot
heiter	bright
herrlich	glorious
kalt	cold
mild	mild
naß	wet
neblig	foggy
regnerisch	rainy
schlecht	bad
schwül	humid
sonnig	sunny
stürmisch	stormy
trocken	dry
trüb	dull
warm	warm
windig	windy

Es blitzt.	It's lightning.
Es donnert.	It's thundering.
Es friert.	It's freezing.
Es hagelt.	It's hailing.
Es nieselt.	It's drizzling.
Es regnet.	It's raining.
Es schneit.	It's snowing.

die Wettervorhersage (n)	weather forecast
der Frost	frost
der Himmel	sky
der Hochdruck	high pressure
der Nebel	fog
der Regen (-)	rain
der Schatten	shade
der Schauer (-)	shower
der Schnee	snow
der Sonnenschein	sunshine
der Sturm ("e)	storm
der Tiefdruck	low pressure
der Wind (e)	wind
die Hitze	heat
die Kälte	cold
die Temperatur (en)	temperature
das Glatteis	black ice
das Klima	climate
minus/plus	minus/plus
niederschlagsfrei	dry
vereinzelt	scattered
zeitweise	at times
Wie ist das Wetter?	What's the weather like?

Und noch etwas...

der Meteorologe (n)/die Meteorologin (nen) — er/sie macht die
   Wettervorhersage

der Regenbogen (¨) — Farbstreifen im Himmel, wenn die Sonne scheint
   und es regnet

das Sauwetter — schreckliches Wetter

es regnet in Strömen — es regnet stark

die Hitzewelle (n) — wenn es für längere Zeit sehr, sehr heiß ist

30 Grad — 30°

auf dem Land   in the country

1 der Baum (¨e)
2 der Berg (e)
3 der Fluß (Flüsse)
4 der See (n)
5 der Wald (¨er)
6 die Blume (n)
7 das Feld (er)

Lerntip!

In a spare moment, it can be useful (and fun!) to imagine a scene and try to think of as many German words for that scene as possible. You might imagine a country scene or a busy town scene, or a classroom or a youth club . . . the list is endless! Look up a couple of words you're not sure of each time and you'll soon increase your vocabulary!

---

der Bach (¨e)   stream
der Bauernhof (-höfe)   farmhouse

der Gipfel (-)	peak
der Hügel (-)	hill
die Gegend (en)	area
die Pflanze (n)	plant
die Landschaft (en)	landscape
die Ruhe	peace
die Umgebung (en)	surrounding area
die Wiese (n)	meadow
das Dorf (¨er)	village
das Gebiet (e)	area
das Landleben (-)	country life
das Tal (¨er)	valley
flach	flat
hügelig	hilly
isoliert	isolated

an der Küste

on the coast

der Liegestuhl (¨e)	deck chair
der Pier (s)	pier
der Sand	sand
der Strand (¨e)	beach
der Strandkorb (-körbe)	beach seat made of wicker
die Düne (n)	dune
die Insel (n)	island
die Möwe (n)	seagull
die Sandburg (en)	sandcastle
die See (n)	sea
das Hochwasser (Flut)	high tide
das Meer (e)	sea
das Niedrigwasser (Ebbe)	low tide
das Seegras	seaweed
die Gezeiten (pl)	tide

die Umwelt	**environment**
der Abfall (-fälle)	rubbish
der Glascontainer (-)	bottle bank
der Grüngürtel (-)	green belt
der Komposthaufen (-)	compost heap
der Müll	rubbish
der grüne Punkt	green dot (on some packaging)
der saure Regen	acid rain
der Regenwald (¨er)	rain forest
der Smog	smog
der Treibhauseffekt (e)	greenhouse effect
der Umweltschutz	environmental protection
der Walfang	whale hunting
die Mehrwegflasche (n)	re-usable bottle
die Umweltverschmutzung	environmental pollution
die Zerstörung	destruction
das Altpapier (e)	waste paper
das Naturschutzgebiet (e)	nature reserve
das Ozonloch	hole in the ozone layer
bedroht	threatened
geschützt	protected
industriell	industrial
umweltfreundlich	environmentally-friendly
verschmutzt	polluted
den Abfall trennen	to sort the rubbish
Energie sparen	to save energy
recyceln	to recycle
schädigen	to damage
schützen	to protect

WÖRTERSPIEL

[A] Write the English meaning to these words and fit them into the grid.

der Schauer = shower

a *die Umwelt* _ _ _ _ _ _ _ _ _ _ _

b *trocken* _ _ _

c *bedeckt* _ _ _ _ _ _ _ _

d *kalt* _ _ _ _

e *das Land* _ _ _ _ _ _ _

f *der Bauernhof* _ _ _ _ _ _ _ _ _

g *die Landschaft* _ _ _ _ _ _ _ _ _

h *der Müll* _ _ _ _ _ _ _

i *sonnig* _ _ _ _ _

j *das Klima* _ _ _ _ _ _ _

k *der Regenbogen* _ _ _ _ _ _ _

l *Blumen* _ _ _ _ _ _ _

m *die Möwe* _ _ _ _ _ _ _

n *die Hitzewelle* _ _ _ _ _ _ _ _

o *verschmutzt* _ _ _ _ _ _ _ _

p *der Strand* _ _ _ _ _

q *Bäume* _ _ _ _ _

S H O W E R

[B] Work with a small group of friends. One of you starts to draw a word or phrase from this unit. The others have to name the word in German. The first person to do so can then choose the next word to draw.

17

At work

die Stelle (n), die Arbeit (en)   job

der   die

Arbeiter (-)	Arbeiterin (nen)	worker
Bauarbeiter (-)	Bauarbeiterin (nen)	builder
Bauer (-)	Bäuerin (nen)	farmer
Berater (-)	Beraterin (nen)	adviser
Buchhalter (-)	Buchhalterin (nen)	accountant
Bürgermeister (-)	Bürgermeisterin (nen)	mayor/ess
Direktor (-)	Direktorin (nen)	headteacher
Gärtner (-)	Gärtnerin (nen)	gardener
Hausmeister (-)	Hausmeisterin (nen)	caretaker
Kellner (-)	Kellnerin (nen)	waiter/waitress
Lehrer (-)	Lehrerin (nen)	teacher
Mechaniker (-)	Mechanikerin (nen)	mechanic
Musiker (-)	Musikerin (nen)	musician
Programmierer (-)	Programmiererin (nen)	programmer
Rentner (-)	Rentnerin (nen)	pensioner
Sänger (-)	Sängerin (nen)	singer
Schaffner (-)	Schaffnerin (nen)	conductor (bus, etc.)
Schauspieler (-)	Schauspielerin (nen)	actor/actress
Schriftsteller (-)	Schriftstellerin (nen)	writer
Sekretär (-)	Sekretärin (nen)	secretary
Verkäufer (-)	Verkäuferin (nen)	sales assistant
Vertreter (-)	Vertreterin (nen)	representative

Fachmann (Fachleute)	Fachfrau	expert
Geschäftsmann (Geschäftsleute)	Geschäftsfrau	business man/woman
Hausmann (-männer)	Hausfrau (en)	house husband/wife
Assistent (en)	Assistentin (nen)	assistant
Chirurg (en)	Chirurgin (nen)	surgeon
Journalist (en)	Journalistin (nen)	journalist
Polizist (en)	Polizistin (nen)	police officer
Beamte (n)	Beamtin (nen)	official
Chef (s)	Chefin (nen)	boss
Friseur (e)	Friseuse (n)	hairdresser
Koch (¨e)	Köchin (nen)	cook
Rechtsanwalt (-anwälte)	Rechtsanwältin (nen)	lawyer
Arzt (¨e)	Ärztin (nen)	doctor
Tierarzt (¨e)	Tierärztin (nen)	vet
Zahnarzt (-ärzte)	Zahnärztin (nen)	dentist
Krankenpfleger (-)	Krankenschwester (n)	nurse

die Arbeitstelle (n)   job

man arbeitet ...	you work ...
in der Bank	at the bank
in einem Büro	in an office
in einem Geschäft	in a shop
in einem Restaurant	in a restaurant
in einer Fabrik	in a factory
für eine Firma	for a company
an/in der Schule	at school
zu Hause	at home
draußen	outside
drinnen	inside

Und noch etwas...

der/die Angestellte (n) — jemand, der arbeitet

der Arbeitgeber (-) — jemand, der anderen eine Arbeit gibt

der Job (s) — die Arbeit

die Teilzeitbeschäftigung (en) — wenn man nicht die ganze Woche arbeitet

das Arbeitsamt (-ämter) — staatliches Büro, das Stellen vermittelt

arbeitslos — wenn man keine Stelle hat

selbständig — wenn man für sich selber arbeitet

berufsunfähig — man kann nicht arbeiten

die Bewerbung (en)	application
der Beruf (e)	profession
der Betrieb (e)	business
der Bewerbungsbrief (e)	letter of application
der Lebenslauf (¨e)	CV
der Lehrling (e)	apprentice
der Lohn (¨e)	wage
der Schichtdienst (e)	shift work
der Termin (e)	appointment
die Berufsberatung	careers advice
die Verabredung (en)	meeting
das Gehalt (¨er)	salary
das Interview (s)	interview
die Arbeitsstunden (pl)	working hours
die Aufstiegschancen (pl)	prospects
die Überstunden (pl)	overtime
sich bewerben für	to apply for
befördet werden	to get promoted
berufstätig sein	to be employed
verdienen	to earn

Lerntip!

Follow this sequence when you learn vocabulary:
- LOOK at the German and English words in the list
- COVER the German words up
- WRITE the German words down on a piece of paper
- CHECK your words against the list.

WÖRTERSPIEL

[A] Label these job pictures. Then cross out the letters in the grid. Can you find two more jobs from the letters left over?

a *Ärztin*

b — — — — — — — —

c — — — — —

d — — — — — — —

e — — — — —

f — — — —

g — — — — — — —

b	ä	p	z	e	k	e	s	i	i	r	t	r	n	l
l	r	h	p	t	e	h	r	ö	c	c	z	l	m	u
e	h	k	a	i	n	h	c	n	k	i	r	t	i	e
l	r	o	o	i	h	i	a	r	n	e	i	n	o	e

[B] Work in a small group. One of you mimes a job. Who can name the German word (both the female and the male form) first? That person can then mime another job.

18

Communications

der Computer (-)   computer

1   der Bildschirm (e)
2   der Drucker (-)
3   der Joystick
4   der Scanner (-)
5   die Diskette (n)
6   die Festplatte (n)
7   die Maus (¨e)
8   die Tastatur (en)
9   das Modem (s)

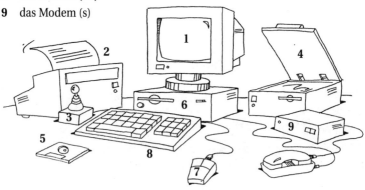

der Cursor (s)	cursor
der Laptop (s)	laptop
der PC	PC
der Programmfehler (-)	bug
der Speicher	memory
der Taschenrechner (-)	calculator
der Virus (Viren)	virus

der Zusammenbruch	crash
die Datenbank (en)	database
die E-Mail (s)	E-mail
die Hardware	hardware
die Software	software
die Taste (n)	key
die Textverarbeitung	word processing
das CD-ROM (s)	CD-Rom
das Dokument (e)	document
das Kennwort ("er)	password
das Menü (s)	menu
das Netzwerk (e)	network
das Notebook (s)	notebook
das Programm (e)	program
das System	system
ab/melden	to log off
an/klicken	to click on
an/melden	to log on
aus/drucken	to print out
Datenkopien erstellen	to back up
drücken	to press
ein/tippen	to key in
formatieren	to format
initialisieren	to initialize
kopieren	to copy
laden	to load
löschen	to erase
programmieren	to program
sichern	to save

Lerntip!

Look at how many words in this section look like their English meaning. That makes them a lot easier to learn.

das Spiel (e)	**game**
der Spieler (-)	player (male)
die Simulation	simulation
die Spielerin (nen)	player (female)
die Stufe (n)	level
das Abenteuerspiel (e)	adventure game
das Computerspiel (e)	computer game
das Videospiel (e)	video game
das Ziel (e)	aim
die Grafiken (pl)	graphics
computersüchtig	addicted to computers
geschickt	skilful
interaktiv	interactive

Und noch etwas...

der Anwender (-)/die Anwenderin (nen) — die Person, die einen Computer benutzt

computerunterstütztes Lernen — wenn man mit Hilfe des Computers lernt

der Heimcomputer (-) — ein Computer, den man zu Hause hat

die Multimediatechnik — die Technik des Computers, des CD-ROMs, usw.

die Raubkopie (n) — eine illegale Kopie

die Spielsoftware — Programme mit Spielen

das Telefon (e)	**phone**
der Anruf (e)	call
der Anrufbeantworter (-)	answerphone
die Direktwahl (en)	direct line
die Leitung (en)	line
die Telefonnummer (n)	phone number
die Telefonkarte (n)	phonecard
die Telefonzelle (n)	phone box

die Verbindung (en)	connection
die Vorwahlnummer (n)	code
das Ferngespräch (e)	long distance call
das Mobiltelefon (e), das Handy	mobile phone
das Ortsgespräch (e)	local call
das R-Gespräch (e)	reverse charge call
das Telefonbuch (-bücher)	phone directory
per Fax	by fax
besetzt	engaged
ab/heben	to pick up
an/rufen	to ring up
auf/legen	to hang up
klingeln, läuten	to ring
telefonieren	to phone
(falsch) wählen	to dial (the wrong number)
Kann ich bitte X sprechen?	Can I speak to X, please?
Kann ich etwas ausrichten?	Can I take a message?
Kann ich bitte eine Nachricht hinterlassen?	Can I leave a message, please?
Hier spricht Y.	It's Y here.
Ich versuche nochmal später.	I'll try again later.
Auf Wiederhören.	Goodbye.

auf der Post — at the post office

der Absender (-)	sender
der Brief (c)	letter
der Briefkasten (¨)	letter box
der Briefträger (-)	postman
der Schalter (-)	counter
der Telebrief (e)	telegram
der Umschlag (-schläge)	envelope
die Adresse (n)	address

die Briefmarke (n)	stamp
die Briefträgerin (nen)	postwoman
die Luftpost	airmail
die Post	post
die Postkarte (n)	postcard
die Postleitzahl (en)	postcode
das Päckchen (-)	small package
das Paket (e)	parcel
das Postamt (-ämter)	post office
das Postwertzeichen (-)	postmark
das Inland	inland
auf/geben	to post
liefern	to deliver
schicken	to send
Sehr geehrter Herr X,	Dear Mr X,
Sehr geehrte Frau Y,	Dear Mrs Y,
Lieber Hans/Liebe Elsa	Dear Hans/Elsa
hochachtungsvoll	yours sincerely
mit freundlichen Grüßen	with best wishes

WÖRTERSPIEL

[A] Look at these English words. How many of the German words for these things are spelled exactly the same?

Joystick Graphics Modem Disc Telephone Software Scanner Menu Network Home computer

[B] Chain game

Play this game with a partner. You say a word from this unit. Your partner then has to say a word starting with the last letter of your word. Who can say the last word?

A: *Computer*
B: *Raubkopie*
A: *eintippen*
B: *Network*
A: *klicken* . . .

am Schalter   at the counter

Can you make up a similar dialogue with a partner?

19

Media

die Unterhaltung (en) entertainment

1 der Fernseher (-)
2 der CD-Spieler (-)
3 der Walkman (s)
4 die CD (s)
5 die Kassette (n)
6 die Schallplatte (n)
7 die Stereoanlage (n)
8 die Zeitung (en)
9 das Radio (s)
10 das Videogerät (e)
11 der Kassettenrecorder (-)

das Fernsehen (-)	**television**
der Dokumentarfilm (e)	documentary
der Moderator (en)	presenter (male)
der Krimi (s)	thriller
der Sender (-)	channel
der Trickfilm (e)	cartoon
die Fernbedienung	remote control
die Komödie (n)	comedy
die Moderatorin (nen)	presenter (female)
die Musiksendung (en)	music show
die Seifenoper (n)	soap opera
die Sendung (en)	show
die Serie (n)	series
die Quizsendung (en)	quiz show
die Wettervorhersage (n)	weather forecast
das Kabelfernsehen (-)	cable television
das Programm (e)	programme
das Satellitenfernsehen (-)	satellite television
die Nachrichten (pl)	news

Lerntip!

Whenever you come across new words, write them down in your vocabulary file or book. But don't just forget them after that – keep on going back and checking yourself on them.

das Lesen	**reading**
der Absatz (-sätze)	paragraph
der Held (en)	hero
der Roman (e)	novel
der Satz (¨e)	sentence
der Titel (-)	title
die Biographie (n)	biography

die Geschichte (n)	story, plot
die Hauptfigur (en)	main character
die Heldin (nen)	heroine
die Illustrierte (n)	colour magazine
die Zeitschrift (en)	magazine
das Bild (er)	picture
das Buch (¨er)	book
das Comic-Heft (e)	comic
das Foto (s)	photo
das Gedicht (e)	poem
das Sachbuch (-bücher)	non-fiction book
das Taschenbuch (-bücher)	paperback
das Theaterstück (e)	play
es handelt sich von . . .	it's about . . .
lesen	to read

das Kino (s); das Theater (-)   cinema; theatre

der Abenteuerfilm (e)	adventure film
der Ausgang (-gänge)	exit
der Eingang (¨e)	entrance
der Eintritt	entry
der Film (e)	film
der Horrorfilm (e)	horror film
der Liebesfilm (e)	love film
der Platz (¨e)	seat
der Rang	circle
die Aufführung (en)	performance
die Bühne (n)	stage
die Ermäßigung (en)	reduction
die Kasse (n)	ticket office
die Karte (n)	ticket
die Matinee (n)	matinée
die Pause (n)	interval

die Vorstellung (en)	showing
das Parkett	stalls
die Karten besorgen	to get the tickets
ausverkauft	sold out

die Werbung	**adverts**
der Slogan (s)	slogan
die Anzeige (n)	advert (in paper)
die Reklame (n)	advert
das Poster (-)	poster

WÖRTERSPIEL

Work out the coded words and write their English meaning.

a *4b 2c 5a 4c 3a 6c 5b*

— — — — — —

b *2a 1a 5a 5c 5a*

— — — — —

c *6b 2c 6c 6a 3a 6c 5b*

— — — — — —

d *5b 2c 6a 5a 7a 4a 4c*

— — — — — — —

e *1a 1b 5c 1c 6c*

— — — — —

f *1c 3a 6b 5b 1c 6c 5b*

— — — — — — —

g *7b 3c 1c 4c 4b*

— — — — —

	1	2	3	4	5	6	7
a	r	k	u	h	i	d	c
b	o	v	x	z	g	s	p
c	a	e	l	t	m	n	w

Make some more coded words for a partner to solve.

20

Current affairs

die Nachrichten (pl)	**the news**
der Flüchtling (e)	refugee
der Frieden	peace
der Kanzler (-)	chancellor
der Krieg (e)	war
der Mord (e)	murder
der Premierminister (-)	prime minister (male)
der Rassismus	racism
der Straßenraub	mugging
der Streik (s)	strike
der Terrorismus	terrorism
die Arbeitslosigkeit	unemployment
die Atomwaffe (n)	nuclear weapon
die Ausländerfeindlichkeit	hostility to foreigners
die Bevölkerung (en)	population
die Bombe (n)	bomb
die Demonstration (en)	demonstration
die Droge (n)	drug
die Entführung (en)	kidnapping
die Europäische Union	European Union
die Flut (en)	flood

die Gesellschaft (en)	society
die Gewalt	violence
die Hungersnot (-nöte)	famine
die Katastrophe (n)	catastrophe
die Krankheit (en)	disease
die Politik	politics
die Premierministerin (nen)	prime minister (female)
die Regierung (en)	government
die Vergewaltigung (en)	rape
die Verhaftung (en)	arrest
die Wahl (en)	election
das Opfer	victim
das Verbrechen (-)	crime
protestieren	to protest

WÖRTERSPIEL

Fill in the gaps.

a *Es gibt eine ..... in Somalia – es gibt nichts zu essen.*
b *Heute gibt es eine ..... gegen Ausländerfeindlichkeit.*
c *Morgen ist Wahltag. Vielleicht gibt es dann eine neue ......*
d *Es gibt keine Stellen in dieser Stadt. ...... ist ein echtes Problem.*
e *Es hat vier Wochen lang nur geregnet. Es gibt eine schreckliche ...... hier.*

21

Adjectives

Positives	positive things
angenehm	pleasant
ansprechend	appealing
auffällig	striking
ausgezeichnet	excellent
beliebt	popular
berühmt	famous
besser	better
einfach	easy
empfehlenswert	recommendable
erfolgreich	successful
erstklassig	first class
es geht	it's OK
fabelhaft	marvellous
fantastisch	fantastic
großartig	splendid
gut	good
interessant	interesting
komisch	funny, strange
lustig	funny
modern	modern
modisch	fashionable
perfekt	perfect
pfiffig	lively
reich	rich
schick	chic
spannend	exciting
toll	great
wunderbar	wonderful

Negatives	negative things
altmodisch	old fashioned
anstrengend	tiring
ärgerlich	irritating
arm	poor
blöd	stupid
brutal	brutal
deprimierend	depressing
doof	stupid
dreckig	dirty
ekelhaft	disgusting
fad	dull
katastrophal	catastrophic
kompliziert	complicated
langweilig	boring
laut	loud, noisy
schlecht, schlimm	bad
schrecklich	awful
schwierig	difficult
stereotyp	stereotypical
traurig	sad
unangenehm	unpleasant

Lerntip!

Lots of adjectives have opposites – *alt/neu, groß/klein* – so try and learn these words together.

die Farbe (n)	colour
blau	blue
blond	blond
braun	brown
gelb	yellow
gold	gold
grau	grey
grün	green
orange	orange
rosa	pink
rot	red
schwarz	black
violett	violet
weiß	white
bunt	colourful
dunkel	dark
gestreift	striped
hell	light
kariert	checked

die Größe (n)	size
ähnlich	similar
breit	wide
dünn	slim
eng	narrow
enorm	enormous
flach	flat, shallow
groß	tall, big
hoch	high
klein	short, small
kurz	short
lang	long
langsam	slow
leicht	light

niedrig	low
schlank	slim
schmal	narrow
schnell	fast
schwach	weak
schwer	heavy
stark	strong
tief	deep
winzig	tiny

Nützliches / **useful words**

besonders	specially
bestimmt	certainly
entweder . . . oder . . .	either . . . or . . .
extrem	extremely
fast	almost
gar nicht	not at all
genauso . . . als . . .	just as . . . as . . .
nicht	not
sehr	very
so	so
total	totally
wahnsinnig	extremely
weder . . . noch . . .	neither . . . nor
weniger	less
wirklich	really
ziemlich	quite
alle	all
also	therefore
andere	other
auch	also
einige	several
gewiß	certain
glücklicherweise	fortunately

hoffentlich	hopefully
kaum	hardly
keine	none
leider	unfortunately
manche	some
mehr	more
natürlich	naturally
nichts	nothing
nur	only
sicher	certainly
sogar	even
sonst	otherwise
ungefähr	about
vielleicht	perhaps
wahrscheinlich	probably
zusammen	together
zuviel	too much
(zu) viele	(too) many

WÖRTERSPIEL

[A] Colour in the shapes in the following order and see which adjective you spell: *red, blue, pink, black, brown, light blue, grey, yellow, gold, violet, green, white.*

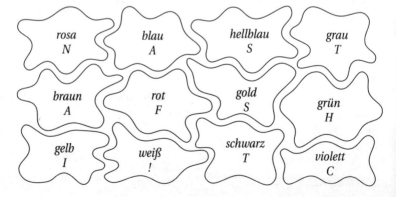

rosa · N
blau · A
hellblau · S
grau · T
braun · A
rot · F
gold · S
grün · H
gelb · I
weiß · !
schwarz · T
violett · C

[**B**] Match the opposites. One opposite is missing. What is it?

teuer	schlecht
intelligent	altmodisch
einfach	schwierig
schmal	weiß
glücklich	fleißig
kurz	breit
niedrig	traurig
faul	hoch
modern	alt
gut	lang
groß	billig
jung	dumm
interessant	dünn
schwarz	langweilig
dick	

22

Verbs

●●● When you use a verb, you need to know the pattern it follows. Some verbs, especially common ones, have irregular patterns in different tenses. Therefore, it is important to check in your course book or at the back of a good dictionary to see which pattern the verb follows.

important verbs

arbeiten	to work
bekommen, kriegen	to get
bleiben	to stay
denken	to think
essen	to eat
geben	to give
gehen	to walk
fahren	to drive
finden	to find
fragen	to ask
haben	to have
helfen	to help
hören	to listen, hear
kaufen	to buy
kommen	to come
lesen	to read
machen	to make
nehmen	to take
sagen	to say
schreiben	to write
sein	to be
sehen	to see
spielen	to play

sprechen	to speak
tragen	to carry, wear
trinken	to drink
werden	to become
wohnen	to live

Lerntip!

Don't be daunted by the amount of verbs to learn! Try and learn them in small groups – just a few at a time. You could make a pairs game to help you. Write the German word on one piece of card and the English meaning on another. Now, set yourself a challenge against the clock: mix up the cards and see how quickly you can match all the pairs. As you learn more verbs, so you can add more cards to your game. Why not play with a partner and see who can get the most pairs?

verbs of action

bauen	to build
besuchen, besichtigen	to visit
brechen	to break
brennen	to burn
bringen	to bring
drehen	to turn
drücken	to push
fallen	to fall
fangen	to catch
holen	to fetch
laufen	to run
öffnen	to open
passieren	to happen
reisen	to travel
schlagen	to beat
suchen	to look for
stecken, stellen	to put

stören	to disturb
treffen	to meet, hit
überqueren	to cross over
verlassen	to leave
verstecken	to hide
wachsen	to grow
ziehen	to pull

verbs of feeling

bedauern	to regret
enttäuschen	to disappoint
(etwas) gern haben	to like (something)
fühlen	to feel
gefallen	to please
hassen	to hate
hoffen	to hope
lachen	to laugh
lächeln	to smile
leiden	to suffer
lieben	to love
vergessen	to forget
vermissen	to miss
weinen	to cry

other verbs

antworten	to reply
beginnen	to begin
benutzen	to use
besprechen	to discuss
danken	to thank
dauern	to last
empfehlen	to recommend
enden	to end
erkennen	to recognize

erklären	to explain
erzählen	to tell
feiern	to celebrate
gucken	to look
halten	to hold
heißen	to be called
kennen	to know (a person)
kleben	to stick
klopfen	to knock
kosten	to cost
leben	to live
leihen	to lend
merken	to notice
mieten	to rent
mogeln	to cheat
organisieren	to organize
nennen	to name
raten	to advise
rauchen	to smoke
reden	to talk
rufen	to call
scheinen	to seem
schicken	to send
schlafen	to sleep
schweigen	to be quiet
stammen aus	to come from
stehlen	to steal
streiten	to argue
üben	to practise
überprüfen	to check
übersetzen	to translate
unterschreiben	to sign
unterstützen	to support
verbessern	to improve

versuchen	to try
wählen	to choose
warten	to wait
wiegen	to weigh
wissen	to know (a fact)
zählen	to count
zeigen	to show

separable verbs

ab/fahren	to depart
an/bieten	to offer
an/fangen	to begin
an/kommen	to arrive
an/machen	to turn on
an/nehmen	to accept
an/sehen	to watch
auf/hören	to stop
auf/machen	to open
aus/füllen	to fill out
aus/machen	to turn off
aus/sehen	to look, appear
ein/gehen	to enter
ein/laden	to invite
kennen/lernen	to get to know
mit/nehmen	to take with you
stehen/bleiben	to stop
vor/schlagen	to suggest
vor/ziehen	to prefer
weiter/gehen	to continue
zurück/kommen	to come back

reflexive verbs

sich amüsieren	to enjoy yourself
sich aus/spannen	to relax

sich aus/ruhen	to rest
sich bedanken	to thank
sich beeilen	to hurry
sich befinden	to be found
sich beschäftigen mit	to be busy with
sich beschweren über	to complain about
sich erinnern an	to remember
sich erkundigen nach	to enquire about
sich heiraten	to get married
sich hin/setzen	to sit down
sich interessieren für	to be interested in
sich langweilen	to be bored
sich sonnen	to sunbathe
sich um/drehen	to turn round
sich verkleiden	to dress up (in fancy dress)

modal verbs

dürfen	to be allowed to
können	to be able to
mögen	to like to
müssen	to have to
sollen	ought to
wollen	to want to

WÖRTERSPIEL

Think of a topic such as:
- *your hobbies*
- *shopping*
- *at school*
- *in a hotel*
- *around the home*

Make a list of all the verbs which would be useful in that situation.
How many verbs can you think of for each one? Compare your list with your partner's.

Answers

1 p.10

a Ich habe mein Heft zu Hause gelassen.

b Was bedeutet »Fußballweltmeisterschaft«?

c Es tut mir leid, daß ich zu spät komme.

d Können Sie bitte langsamer sprechen?

e Darf ich aufs Klo gehen?

f Wie buchstabiert man »Bahnhof«?

g Darf ich das Fenster aufmachen?

2 p.17

a) acht, b) Freitag, c) Juli, d) fünfzig, e) Herbst, f) siebte, g) halb sieben

3 p.23

[**A**] Cousine (cousin), Einzelkind (only child), Enkelin (granddaughter), Großvater (grandfather), Halbbruder (half brother), intelligent (intelligent), Religion (religion), schüchtern (shy), Stiefbruder (stepbrother), Tante (aunt), Witwer (widower)

p.24

[**B**] der Familienname (surname), der Vorname (first name), das Geschlecht (sex), männlich/weiblich (male/female), die Adresse (address), die Postleitzahl (postcode), die Telefonnummer (phone number), das Geburtsdatum (date of birth), das Alter (age), der Geburtsort (place of birth), der Wohnort (place of residence), die Staatsangehörigkeit (nationality), die Religion (religion), evangelisch/katholisch (evangelical/catholic), die Unterschrift (signature)

4 p.27

1b Katze, 2a Maus, 3e Kuh, 4d Ziege, 5c Fisch

5 p.33

1b, 2a, 3c, 4b

7 p.42

sich rasieren, aufstehen, frühstücken, bügeln, kehren, sich duschen, kochen, sich anziehen – ausgehen

8 p.48

der Kugelschreiber (-) (pen), Erdkunde (geography), das Klassenzimmer (-) (classroom), Chemie (chemistry), der Schulhof (-höfe) (playground), der Filzstift (e) (felt tip pen), Kunst (art), die Gesamtschule (n) (comprehensive school), die Klasse (n) (class), der Direktor (-) (headmaster), die Lehrerin (nen) (female teacher), das Labor (e) (lab), Sport (sport), Mathe (maths), das Lineal (e) (ruler)

9 p.56

Aprikose, Bohne

10 p.61

Jogginganzug, Pfandflasche, Supermarkt, Blumengeschäft, Gummistiefel, Kaufhaus, Zeitungskiosk, Badehose

12 p.74

[A] a) mit dem Rad, b) mit dem Zug, c) mit dem Auto, d) mit dem Motorrad, e) mit der Fähre, f) zu Fuß, g) mit dem Hubschrauber, h) mit der Straßenbahn

[B] a) to cycle, b) to brake, c) to steer, d) to drive, e) to pack, f) to close, g) to be late, h) to wait, i) to appear, shine, j) to eat, k) to secure, l) to depart

13 p.80

[A] a) Italien, b) Griechenland, c) Deutschland, d) Rußland, e) Deutschland, f) Österreich, g) die Schweiz

[**B**] a) 16, b) Baden-Württemberg, c) Mecklenburg-Vorpommern, d) ja,
e) nein, in Sachsen, f) Main

16 p.97
a) environment, b) dry, c) overcast, d) cold, e) country, f) farmhouse,
g) landscape, h) rubbish, i) sunny, j) climate, k) rainbow, l) flowers,
m) seagull, n) heatwave, o) polluted, p) beach, q) trees

17 p.101
a) Ärztin, b) Polizistin, c) Köchin, d) Mechaniker, e) Bauer, f) Pilot,
g) Lehrerin – Koch/Lehrer

18 p.107
Joystick, Modem, Software, Scanner

19 p.111
a) Zeitung (newspaper), b) Krimi (thriller), c) Sendung (programme),
d) Gedicht (poem), e) Roman (novel), f) Ausgang (exit), g) Platz (seat)

20 p.113
a) Hungersnot, b) Demonstration, c) Regierung/Premierministerin,
d) Arbeitslosigkeit, e) Flut

21 p.118

[**A**] fantastisch!

p.119

[**B**] intelligent/dumm, einfach/schwierig, schmal/breit, glücklich/traurig,
kurz/lang, niedrig/hoch, faul/fleißig, modern/altmodisch, gut/schlecht,
jung/alt, interessant/langweilig, schwarz/weiß, dick/dünn,
teuer/billig – groß/klein